# Computer networking beginners guide

## Ultimate guide to master communication system including cisco and ccna, wireless and cloud technology, system security administration and ip subnetting

**[Ramon Base]**

**Legal & Disclaimer**

The information contained in this book and its contents is not designed to replace or take the place of any form of medical or professional advice; and is not meant to replace the need for independent medical, financial, legal or other professional advice or services, as may be required. The content and information in this book has been provided for educational and entertainment purposes only.

The content and information contained in this book has been compiled from sources deemed reliable, and it is accurate to the best of the Author's knowledge, information and belief. However, the Author cannot guarantee its accuracy and validity and cannot be held liable for any errors and/or omissions. Further, changes are periodically made to this book as and when needed. Where appropriate and/or necessary, you must consult a professional (including but not limited to your doctor, attorney, financial advisor or such other professional advisor) before using any of the suggested remedies, techniques, or information in this book.

# Table of Contents

# Introduction

You might have heard about wireless access points, wireless networking, and wireless computing. These are different terms that are all related to wireless technology. Of course, they are not the only wireless devices; there are a plethora of wireless devices and technologies in the modern era. However, what is wireless technology and what are wireless devices? These and several other related questions will be answered in this chapter. Firstly, let me briefly give you an insight into what wireless technology is.

## What is wireless technology?

Daniel Fuchs, the Head of Innovation at Vodafone and IoT Evangelist, defined wireless technology as "...any technology that allows users to transmit any type of communication like voice, data, and message using the air as the 'conductive' way to transport it."

Thus, it refers to technology that is not powered by wires and physical cables. By implication, wireless technology covers the use of radio frequencies and signals for data transmission rather than the conventional mode of data transmission via cables and the likes. For instance, phone channels, the Internet, and communication use physical wires that are physically connected for data transmission. Thus, rather than follow the physical connection, wireless technologies make the connection of each node of a network to be done with radio waves, thus eliminating the use of cables and other devices used for physical connection.

Another transmission technique that falls in this category is light based-transmission. This is a new wireless technology where light is used as the channel of data transmission in opposition to the use of wires and cables. This technology doesn't depend on the use of physical wires for connection and is thus regarded as a wireless technology.

It is true that wireless communication has been around for over a century; they have been in use since 1876. The astronomical increase in the areas of application of wireless technology today makes it absolutely important to discuss the technology in detail.

Wireless technology has a wide range of applications. It can be adapted for use in different areas of human endeavor, from insurance to education, business to entertainment, and other areas of application.

# Chapter 1: Components of a network

## 1) TCP

**TCP** comes from **T**ransmission **C**ontrol **P**rotocol, and it does exactly what it says: ensures the transmission control of every single packet within a communication channel.

It can be found (together with UDP) on the 4th layer of the OSI model, which is the Transport layer. As a PDU (Protocol Data Unit), **TCP uses segments** (it breaks the data into smaller pieces known as segments).

TCP is a protocol that's being used (by you, me and everyone else on the Internet) all the time (without us even being aware of it). That's because it does a great job in keeping this seamless.

For example, when we download a file from the Internet, or access a web page, or **connect in any way to a network device**, we use the TCP protocol.

Now comes the question: **Why? Why do we need it?** Because TCP allows us to communicate by sharing the exact data (ex: web page) that the server or the client has. So when we download a file (through FTP), the TCP will ensure that **each segment** composing the file (that's located on the server) will be received. In case of missing segments, everything will be retransmitted.

So here are some of the features and benefits of the TCP protocol:

- **Retransmission** of data (in case it's being "lost on the road")

- Packet reordering

- **Establishes a connection** between the client and the server (3-way handshake)

TCP achieves the elements mentioned above by using the following message types:

- SYN, ACK, FIN

- PSH, RST, URG

We'll talk more about them in the following sections. Now let's see how TCP works. In figure 6.1 you can see the **TCP header structure:**

Having all of these fields in the protocol header, TCP can provide us with:

- Data reordering

- **Data retransmission,** in case of packet loss by using **sequence numbers.**

- Reliable applications

**Each packet** (or packet group) has a **sequence number** associated with it. If the recipient receives a certain number of packets (defined by the sequence number), then it will send back an acknowledgement message (ACK) for those (received) packets:

Thus, it's easy for the recipient to figure out what packets have reached and what packets need to be retransmitted. If the source (client) does not receive an ACK for any packets, then it will retransmit those packets.

At first, when two devices want to communicate via a client-server connection, a **3-Way Handshake** session must be established.

How does a Client establish a connection to a Server?

As I said earlier, when a server has to communicate with a client, the two will form a connection between them. This connection is known as the **3-Way Handshake**. Now, let's take a look on how this handshake takes place:

At first, the client (the one who starts the connection) will send to the server:

a synchronisation message (**SYN**) - marking the beginning of a session

The server will respond with an acknowledgement (**SYN-ACK**)

The client will also respond to the server with an acknowledgement (**ACK**)

This way, the **TCP connection** (via **3-way handshake**) between the client and the server was

**established**. Now the two devices can communicate (send web traffic, transfer files, etc.).

This mechanism of the 3-way handshake helps ensure the client and the server that all packets are being counted (sequenced), ordered and verified at their destination. In case some of the packets are missing, they are going to be resent (by the sender).

How does TCP terminate a connection?

After all packets have been transmitted, the connection must end. This is similar to a 3-way handshake, but this time 4 packets are being sent:


**the client** sends a **FIN** packet

**the server** responds with an acknowledgement (**FIN-ACK**)

**the server** also sends a **FIN** message

**the client** replies with an acknowledgement, **FIN-ACK**

And so, the TCP connection between the two devices will end.

15

## 2) UDP (User Datagram Protocol)

**UDP** is the exact opposite of TCP (it doesn't retransmit packets, it doesn't establish a connection before sending data, it doesn't establish the packets etc.). **UDP simply sends** the **packets** from a specific **source** to a specific **destination** without being interested in the connection's status. The **advantage** of using this protocol is the **low latency**, which allows for the smooth transition of the application with the lowest delay possible.

Thus, UDP is **suitable** for **real-time applications** (e.g. Voice, Video traffic) that need to **reach** the **destination as quickly as possible**. In figure 6.8 you can see how the UDP header looks. Compared to TCP, it's much simpler and efficient in processes and bandwidth utilisation.

Because we were talking about real-time applications such as Skype, Facebook, CS Online, here are a few requirements for VoIP (**V**oice **o**ver **IP**), or other similar delay sensitive apps:

- **Delay: < 150 ms:** Open CMD, type ping 8.8.8.8 and see the delay of every packet

- **Packet Loss: < 1%:** 1 second of voice = 50 packets of 20 ms audio each => 1% of 50 = 0,5; (this means that at every 2 seconds we can lose max 1 packet)

- Jitter (variable delay): < 30ms

At the beginning of this chapter I told you that TCP uses segments (as the PDU), but in the case of the UDP protocol things change a little bit. **UDP** does not use segments, it uses **datagrams** (it breaks the data into datagrams which are smaller in size than segments).

Now, let's take another example. In figure 6.10 we can see another type of traffic:

- **DNS queries** (name resolution of a domain to an IP address).

We can see that the DNS protocol uses UDP for data transport, and more specific uses **port 53.** As you can see, I mentioned the term "port". In this case, we are not talking about a physical port (the place where you plug the cable in), but we are referring to a **logical port**, which identifies the *network applications* **that are *running*** on a *device* (be it Router, Server, Laptop etc.).

## 3) Ports

**A port** uniquely identifies a **network application** (Web server, DNS server, etc.) on a device in a network. Each port has an identifier (a number, ranging from **1** to **65535**). When a PC sends a request (for a web page) to a server, this request will contain (among other) the following information:

Source IP: **PC**

Destination IP: **Server**

**Source Port**: 29813 (randomly generated by the Browser)

Destination Port: **80**

In other words: The PC's browser (with a source port of 29813) requests from the server (Destination) a web page (port 80).

**Example #1** - TCP ports

Now let's take a few examples where we can analyse and talk about what we've been discussing in this chapter.

As you can see in Figure 6.11, there is a communication flow between 2 devices (source: 10.0.1.43, destination: 139.61.74.125).

The **source port** (generated randomly) in this case is 55881 (most likely was generated by a browser - Google Chrome, Safari, Firefox, etc.), and the destination port is **443** (**HTTPS**, a secured web application).

Thus, the source addresses are requesting a web page hosted by a server placed somewhere on the Internet. Besides, in the lower half of the figure, you can see the structure of the TCP header with all of its fields that have been shown in figure 6.1.

In this case, we can easily identify the ports, the sequence number of the current packet (segment), the acknowledgement number, the window size and so on.

# Chapter 2: Networking hardware

A **network** is a group of **interconnected** devices (PCs, Laptops, Servers, smartphones, etc.) that can communicate (exchange information) with each other. All of these devices are communicating through special network equipment (**Routers** and **Switches**). We'll talk more about Routers and Switches in later chapters. For now, let's see the existing network types.

1) Network Types

Computer networks can be:

- **MAN – Metropolitan Area Network** – extended network, covering the entire surface of a city

- **WAN – Wide Area Network** – multiple networks (LANs) of an organisation, which are interconnected

- ***WWAN –*** World Wide Area Network **– the Internet**

- **WLAN – Wireless LAN** – aka Wi-Fi, which are usually created by our home Router

- **LAN – Local Area Network** – your home network

In addition to these network types, there are others, of different sizes or purposes (e.g.: SAN - Storage Area Network, EPN – Enterprise Private Network, VPN – Virtual Private Network).

Now let's take a closer look at some of the networks mentioned above:

A **LAN** is a relatively small network that is **local to an organisation** or a home. For example, your home network is considered a LAN because it is limited in terms of the number of devices connected to it.

A school network (although larger than a home network) is considered a LAN because it interconnects many devices (all computers, servers, etc.) in the same network.

Moving forward to the next network type: if we were to combine multiple networks and allow them to interconnect within a city, then we would form a **MAN** (a much wider network, which would be spread across an entire city. This type of network offers **higher transfer speeds** of data than the usual Internet connection).

Now, as I said earlier, a MAN is a network that interconnects multiple networks within a city, The purpose of a **WAN** is to connect the network of multiple cities (or even countries) in order to form a wider network, across a large geographical area. We can also say that **multiple LANs** of an organisation (or multiple organisations) that are interconnected form a WAN.

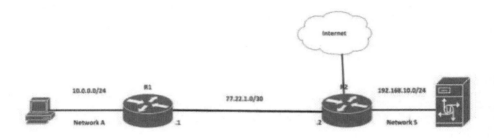

Figure 1.1

**For example**, in figure 1.1 you can see 2 Routers, 1 PC and 1 Server. The connection between the PC and Router R1 forms a LAN (the same for R2 and the Server). The connection between the 2 Routers will form a WAN because they are connecting multiple networks. If you're confused, don't worry! We'll talk about all of these concepts in depth, throughout this book.

A **WLAN** (aka Wi-Fi) is a LAN to which we can connect wireless from our smartphones, tablets, laptops, or any other device. The wireless environment is separate from the physical (cable) one and has different properties in terms of speed, security, coverage, etc. The main benefit of Wireless connectivity is the flexibility that it offers.

2) Network Topologies

In a typical network environment there can be multiple representations of devices. All of these devices can be grouped in multiple ways, considering what different purposes they are serving.

For example, if we only care for network connectivity (or Internet access), we'll group the devices in a **star-like topology**. The problem in this scenario would be the lack of redundancy (a very important part of computer networking).

So, if we intend to have a very reliable network (such as one of an ISP - Internet Service Provider), then we would use a **mesh topology**. Let's take a closer look at the different types of network representations in the figures below:

In figure 1.2 we have the **Star Topology** that we spoke of earlier. The devices that are interconnected are Switches (network devices that connect us to a LAN – and we're going to talk about these in depth, a little bit later). Here's a visual representation of how a network would look like:

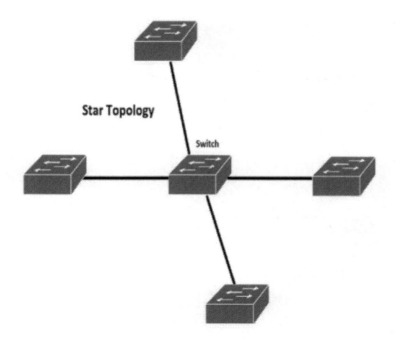

Figure 1.2

Next in our topology design, we have our Switches connected in a **Full Mesh Topology** (figure 1.3). This topology allows for full redundancy. In case something bad happens with a cable or with a Switch, there will be redundant ways to reach the Internet or a different destination.

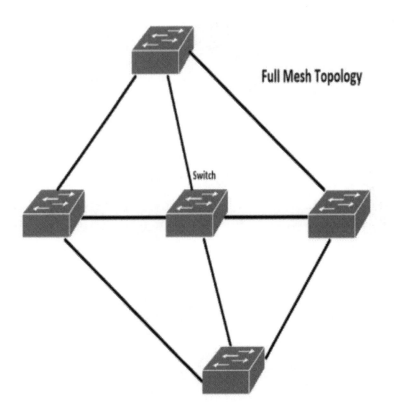

Figure 1.3

Let's not forget that full redundancy requires more devices and more cabling (which implies more money). So, the full mesh topology will be more expensive to implement than the one in figure 1.4

The 3rd topology is **Partial Mesh**. This provides redundancy only for a part of the network (and Switches), while the other Switches are left with a "single way out". This topology is cheaper than the Full Mesh implementation.

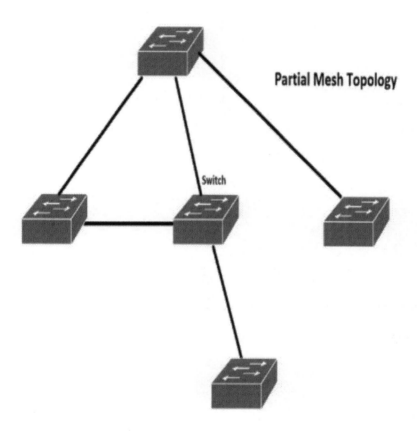

Figure 1.4

And the last but not least is the Hub and Spoke. This one is very often used in the WAN (Internet) design. The 3 Routers in this topology don't know each other, by default, so both R1 and R3 will have to send their data (aka. traffic) to R2, which knows how to redirect the traffic so it will reach its destination.

For example, if R1 wants to send traffic to R3, they will do it by sending it to the Hub (R2), as it knows what to do with it (where to redirect it).

This design is being used because it scales. In this representation we only have 3 Routers, but what are you going to do when you'll have 20, 80, 200? Then it will be very hard to track all of them (or assign manually paths to certain destinations).

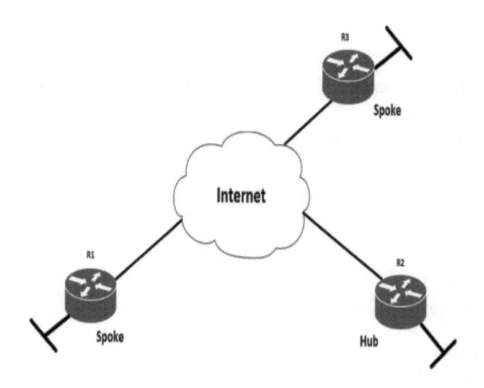

Figure 1.5

3) Network Components

Let's take a closer look at the network components listed above:

## A. END DEVICES & MEANS FOR TRANSMISSION

Generally, we are the ones that have a device (end-device). Each of us has a Laptop, tablet or smartphone with which we connect to the Internet. The connection can be made with 1 or more transmission media means (electricity, light impulses, radio waves).

When we connect with our smart phones to the Internet, we use the wireless connection. If we are on a Laptop

or a PC, we can connect it either wireless, or through a network cable (UTP).


Figure 1.6

We use optical fiber when we want to connect multiple networks or a server equipment (ex. switch - switch, server - switch). The reason is simple: an optical fiber connection is much faster than UTP (cable) or Wireless. We can transfer more data (10, 40, 100 Gbps throughput), on a longer range (1 - 5 km or miles).

Also, optical fiber is now being used regularly when connecting a home user to the Internet. The main reason for this is the fact that optical fiber can transfer data at higher speeds and at a longer distance (1 - 5 miles/km), which is way better than the classic UTP cable that caps out at 100 meters!

## B. SWITCH

A **Switch** (figure 1.7) is a **network device** that **interconnects** multiple end-devices (PCs, laptops, printers, IP phones, Servers etc.) in the same Local Area Network (**LAN**).

It is well known for its **high port density** (generally **24**, **48**, or even more), capable of speeds between 1 Gbps and 10 Gbps (or even 40 Gbps) per port. The switch uses MAC addresses as a way of identifying the end-devices connected to the network (we will talk about this in more detail, in Chapter 4). Here is an image with a Cisco **Switch**:

Figure 1.7

C. ROUTER

A **Router** is a network device that has the role of **interconnecting multiple networks** (LANs) and forming a larger network (**WAN** - Wide Area Network).

The Router is the (main) device that **connects us to the Internet**, through its ability to handle packet delivery from any source (network) to any destination (network).

The Router achieves this by using **IP addresses** in order to identify the source and the destination devices (we'll talk more about IP addresses in Chapter 3).

When comparing it to a Switch, the Router has way fewer ports (between 2 to 5) at similar speeds (100 Mbps - 10Gbps, depending on the model). Bellow you can see a Cisco **Router**:

Figure 1.8

## 4) How can we represent (or "draw") a network?

Usually, networks are being **represented** by a "**network topology**", which can be of 2 types: **logical** or **physical**. Logical topologies describe the logical aspects of a network: the IP addresses of the networks, the way the devices are connected, the routing protocols that are being used, etc. The following example is a logical topology and is composed of 2 Routers, 1 PC, and 1 Server. One of the Routers is connected to the Internet:

Example          #          1          Logical          Topology

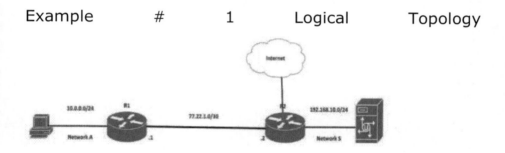

Figure 1.9

In this second example, the network is composed of 1 Switch, 3 Routers, 2 PCs and 1 Server

Example #2 Logical Topology

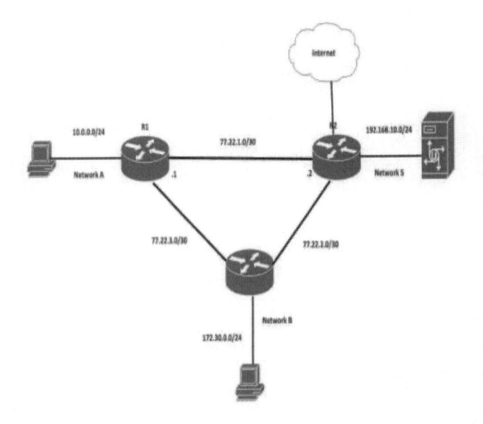

Figure 1.10

**Physical topology** describes the physical aspect of a network: where the devices are placed, what type of cables we are using, how many ports do we need, on what ports/switch will be the servers connected, etc. It actually shows where the equipment is (physically) located, and what is its main purpose within the network.

5) How do computers communicate over the Internet?

In order to communicate (send traffic – aka. connect to Facebook, Google, etc.), the devices (PCs, Routers, Switches, etc.) must have a **unique identifier**. In the Internet world, this identifier is known as **IP (Internet Protocol)**.

The IP is the way we identify a device in a network or on the Internet. **It must be unique**. There can't be 2 equal IP addresses in the same network (or in the Internet), because there will be a conflict and the Internet connection will not work properly. Here are 2 examples of an IP address: 192.168.1.170 or 84.222.0.93

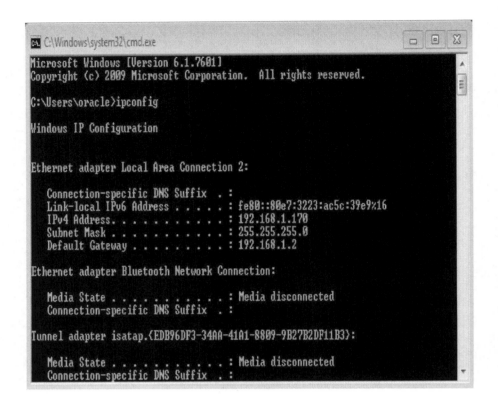

Figure 1.11

In figure 1.11, you can see the command line of Windows (**cmd**). Here's another example of an IP address:

10.0.0.1/24**, where** /24 **is the** network mask

The **subnet mask** determines the **network size** (ex: how many devices can be connected to the same

40

network, at the same time: for /28 there can be no more than 14 devices, in /25 there is a max of 126, for /24 a max of 254 etc.).

Below are the necessary **components** for an end-device to **communicate** (connect) **successfully** on the Internet:

**IP address** = uniquely identifies a device connected to a network

**Network Mask** = determines the size of a network (ex: the number of available IP addresses)

**Default Gateway** = specifies the way out of the network (a Router connected to the Internet)

**DNS Server** = "transforms" a name (i.e. google.com) into an IP address (i.e. 173.23.85.91)

In the next chapter, we are going to talk about the OSI Model, which is a framework broken down into 7 layers that explain exactly how the Internet (and communication) works.

# Chapter 3: wireless hardware and standard

In the previous chapter, I listed security threat as one of the most dangerous challenges of computer networking. This is not unconnected to the havoc that potential cybercriminals can wreck on a network with lax security measures. In this chapter, I will discuss the concept of wireless technology security extensively in order to assist you to have a deeper understanding of the concept, the potential security threats, and the practical security tips that can serve as preventive measures against these threats.

## What is wireless network security?

This is the first question that most people ask. Well, there are different definitions for wireless network security. According to Wikipedia, "wireless security is the prevention of unauthorized access or damage to computers using wireless networks."

This definition by Technopedia also captures the concept well: "Wireless network security is the process of designing, implementing, and ensuring security on a wireless computer network. It is a subset of network security that adds protection for a wireless computer network."

These two definitions have obviously given you a better understanding of wireless network security that is otherwise known as wireless security. Wireless security is designed to protect a wireless network form malicious access attempts by potential hackers as well as from unauthorized personnel. Going by the name, you will realize that wireless network security is also done with a wireless switch/router or other wireless devices that by default can encrypt and secure wireless communication.

Sometimes, the wireless security may be compromised. In that event, the hacker is prevented from viewing the content of the packet or traffic in transit. More so, there are wireless intrusion systems that are responsible for detecting potential intrusions and preventing such an intrusion by alerting the network administrator whenever it detects any security breach.

## Types of wireless network security

The increased global concern about the security of wireless networks has triggered the need for different security measures to be developed with the goal of reinforcing the security of wireless networks. Wireless network security can be achieved through some standards and algorithms that are specifically designed for that purpose. Some of these security measures are:

### Wi-Fi Protected Access (WPA)

The Wi-Fi Protected Access is a security certification and security program for securing wireless computer networks designed to address some of the weaknesses in the Wired Equivalent Privacy (WEP). When you use WPA encryption for securing your Wi-Fi networks, you need a passphrase, otherwise known as a password, or a network security key. The passphrases are usually made up of numbers and letters. To establish a connection to the Wi-Fi network, the computer and whatever other connected devices must use the passphrase.

If you personally own the Wi-Fi network, it is advisable that you choose your own password when setting up the Wi-Fi network. Your password must be lengthy and be made up of alphanumeric characters and special characters to increase the security level of the password to prevent someone without the right authorization access to your network. When choosing a passphrase, you should also ensure that your passphrase is unique and cannot be easily guessed or cracked.

## Wired Equivalent Policy (WEP)

WEP has been around for years. It's one of the security methods that have been around for years, especially for supporting older devices. The WEP security technique is not difficult to implement. You will trigger a network security key whenever you enable the WEP. The security key will encrypt any information that the computer shares with any other computer on the network. WEP was made known to the public by the Institute of Electrical and Electronics Engineers (IEEE) in 1979. This is a not-for-profit organization that has the responsibility of developing the right standards that can be adopted in electronic transmissions. There are two types of WEP. They are:

- **Shared key authentication:** This is a channel through which a computer can access a WEP-based wireless network. If a computer has a wireless modem, SKA will allow it to have access to the WEP network to enable it to exchange both unencrypted and encrypted data. For this authentication type to function efficiently, a wireless access point must match a WEP encryption key that has been obtained prior to the time of use by the connecting computer.

The connection process starts when the computer contacts the access point with an authentication request. In response to the request, the access point will generate a challenge text, a sequence of characters, for the computer. The computer will use its WEP key for encrypting the challenge text and later transmit it to the access point. After receiving the message, the access point will decrypt it and subsequently compare the result of the decrypted message with the main challenge text. If there are no mistakes in the decrypted message, the access point will immediately send the authentication code needed by the connecting computer to the computer. Then, finally, the connecting computer will accept the sent authentication code and thus is integrated into the network throughout the session or throughout the period when the connecting computer is within the original access point's range. On the other hand, if there is a discrepancy between the original text and the decrypted message, the access point will prevent the computer from becoming a part of the network.

- **Open system authentication:** The Open System Authentication (OSA) refers to a technique that allows a computer to gain unrestricted access to a WEP-based wireless network. With this system authentication, any computer that has a wireless modem can gain access to any network where it can receive unencrypted files. For the Open System Authentication to work, the computer's Service Set Identifier (SSID) should be the same with that of the wireless access point. The SSID refers to some well-arranged characters that uniquely assign names to a Wireless Local Area Network. The whole process occurs in just three stages.

First, the computer will send a request to the access point for authentication. When the access point receives the request, it will randomly generate an authentication code that is intended for use at the right time: during the session. Finally, the computer will take the authentication code and thus integrate into the network throughout the duration of the session and as long as the computer is within the range of the access point. You need a Shared Key Authentication (SKA), a better and stronger authentication technique, if you find it necessary to transfer encrypted data between a wireless-equipped computer and the access point of a WEP network.

## Top ways to secure your wireless network

Today, the popularity of wireless networks comes at a price: cybercriminals are always on the lookout for possible loopholes they can exploit to breach your security and compromise your data. Hence, it is a matter of urgency to find some ways to beef the security of your wireless network to prevent these criminals from breaching your security. Here are some security measures that can guarantee the security of your wireless network:

## Understand the principle behind wireless networks

Understanding the principle behind how a wireless network works can be of help in safeguarding your wireless networks. If you want to go wireless, you need to connect a DSL modem, a cable, or any other access point to a wireless router. The router will then send a signal out through the air to the desired destination, which may sometimes be a couple of hundred feet away. Any device that is connected within the range will be able to pull the signal and have access to the Internet. With this understanding, you are likely more willing to take necessary precautions to ensure that no one has access to your network besides yourself and other authorized people.

## Encrypt your wireless network

If you are using a wireless network at home or in your office, make it a point of duty to encrypt any type of information you want to transfer over the network to prevent eavesdroppers from gaining access to your

49

confidential information. When you encrypt a data, it is scrambled into a code that others cannot gain access to. Encrypting your data is obviously the most potent way of shutting out intruders from your network.

There are two encryption techniques for the encryption: WPA and WEP. You should always use the same encryption for your router, computer, and other devices. If you need ideas, give WPA2 a try. This encryption technique is efficient and will secure your network against hackers. If you use wireless routers, they always have their encryption turned off. Turn this feature on to secure your network. You will find how to do this if you go through the router's manual. If you can't find the instruction on the manual, visit the router company's official website for the instruction.

Limit access to your network

It is also your responsibility to ensure that only certain devices are allowed to access your wireless network. All the devices that are able to effectively communicate with a wireless network are automatically assigned a unique MAC (Media Access Control) address. Wireless routers are designed with a mechanism that they use for allowing devices that have specific MAC address to gain access to a network to ensure the security of your network. However, you should be cautious when using this security option. Some hackers and other cybercriminals have found a way to mimic MAC addresses and can easily infiltrate your network. Therefore, complement this security technique with some other effective network security techniques.

Secure your router

Your router is another device that deserves protection as well so that your wireless network won't be susceptible to cyber-attack via some loopholes in the security of your router. It is the responsibility of your router to direct traffic between the Internet and your local network. Therefore, protecting your router is the first step towards the protection of your entire network. If you leave your router unprotected, strangers may gain access to your network and thus access your personal and confidential information such as your financial information. If they have complete control of your router, you can't predict what they will do with your network.

## Change your router's default name

Your router obviously comes with a default name. This name is sometimes called SSID or the service set identifier. This is the name assigned to the router by the manufacturer. To increase the security of your wireless network, it is advisable that you change this default name and give the router a unique and difficult-to-guess name. Also, don't reveal this name to anyone. If you are the only person with access to the default name, it is almost impossible for the router to be subjected to a security breach.

## Change the router's default password(s)

Just as the router comes with a default name, it also comes with a default password or a group of passwords. This password gives you the freedom to set up the router as well as operate it. Hackers are familiar with the default passwords and can use the knowledge to hack your router and gain access to your network if you leave the default password(s) unchanged. Make the password change for both the "administrator" and "user."

The rule of thumb stipulates that you use a combination of letters and numbers, known as alphanumeric characters, as well as long and difficult-to-guess passwords. It is advisable that you use a minimum of 12 characters for your password. You may also include lowercase and uppercase letters. The more complex your password, the more difficult it is for hackers to break. If you are unsure about how to change the password, visit the router company's website, and you will be guided through the process.

## Don't always log in as administrator

After you have successfully set up your router, don't keep yourself logged in as administrator. Rather, you should log out immediately if you are not using the router. This will reduce the risk of being piggybacked on during your session in order to have access to your login details and take control of your router. That may have a dire consequence on your network.

## Turn off "Remote Management" features

The reason for this security measure is pretty obvious. Some routers' manufacturers offer the option to keep the remote management option turned on in order to provide you with technical support when necessary. Sadly, leaving this option turned on is synonymous to making your financial information available to the public. Hackers may capitalize on the feature to gain access to your router and, invariably, your network. On the other hand, when you leave this feature turned off, controlling your network from a remote location is impossible.

Always update your router

In order for your router to work effectively and be secure, the accompanying software must be regularly updated to fix bugs and other issues. Before setting up your router, visit the router's website to see if you can get the updated software that you can download. It is a course of wisdom to register the router with the manufacturer as well as sign up to receive regular updates to ensure that you are kept in the loop whenever there is a new software version.

Secure your computer

Regardless of the security measures you adopt for your router and other devices that are connected to your network, it is imperative that you secure your computer too. For instance, you can use some protections such as antispyware, antivirus, and firewall to fortify the security of your computer. Remember to keep the software up-to-date as well. Some valuable security tips include using a strong password for your computer and using up-to-date antivirus, antispyware, and firewalls. Don't forget to enable 2-factor authentication as well. Read this article: *"**Computer Security**"* for more practical tips that will help you keep your computer safe and secure from potential cybercriminals.

Log out of connected apps

If you access your network via an app, don't keep the app open when you are not using the app. Log out immediately and log in again whenever you want to access the network with the app. Why should you go through this process of logging in and out frequently? Remember that you can lose your phone or have it stolen at any time. Keeping the app open allows others to access your network via the stolen or lost phone. To further increase the security of the network through the app, adopt the password tips. Use a strong password that hackers will have a challenging time hacking so the chances of others gaining access to your network through your app are drastically reduced.

Password your phone

While password-protecting your app is a good idea, think about making your phone inaccessible to others as well. Protecting your phone will create the first barrier against unauthorized access to your phone and your network. I have given a list of practical tips for creating strong and difficult-to-hack passwords. Go through the chapter again and implement the tips. The stronger your password, the more difficult it is to hack your phone and access sensitive information that may be used against you or your network.

Reduce the range of your wireless signal

This is another effective security option you should consider. This is applicable to users whose wireless routers have a very high range while the users are using small spaces for operation. If you are in that group, decrease the signal range. There are two ways to do this. You can either change your wireless channel or change your router's mode to 802.11g rather than the conventional 802.11b or 802.11n. Alternatively, you can place the router in some secluded places such as inside a shoe box or under a bed. You can also wrap a foil around its antennas to perfectly restrict its signals' direction.

Stay under the radar

To hide the visibility of your network and stop your wireless network from broadcasting its presence, disable the router's Service Set Identifier (SSID) to make it "invisible." This will prevent strangers beside your business or home from being aware of the network and its name. This will also reduce the number of people who may be interested in gaining access to your network.

Turn off the network when not in use

This is considered by some experts as "the ultimate in wireless security measures." The reason for this assertion is not far-fetched: if you shut your network down, most hackers will certainly be prevented from breaking in. While it may be impractical to keep switching the network off and on frequently, it is still practical to do it occasionally when you won't be using the network for a long time, perhaps when on vacation or when you will be offline for an extended period of time.

Have antimalware installed on connected devices

It is not out of place to take an inventory of the wide variety of devices connected to the network. When you have a full list of the devices, ensure that they all have antimalware installed on each of the devices for maximum protection against external invasion, especially in devices that can support the protection. Listed above are some effective ways you can close the door to your wireless network to the bad guys and thus prevent your network from being compromised. The suggestions here are practical and very easy to implement.

The tips discussed above have been tested and proven reliable over the years. Since precaution is usually better than cure, taking these steps to boost the security of your network is more rewarding and more effective than waiting until disaster strikes before running from pillar to post looking for a solution to the problem, so increase the immunity of your network and give cybercriminals a second thought about making attempts to breach your security. If you don't implement these tips, you are a sitting duck, an easy target for hackers.

# Chapter 4: Cabling management

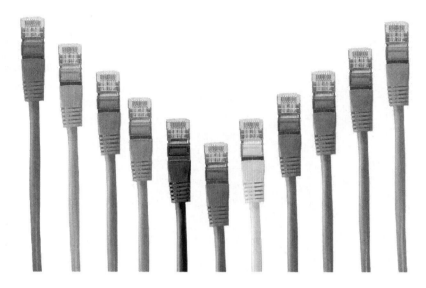

The wireless technology is not the only networking technology. Prior to the advent of the wireless technology, many wired technologies held sway. These technologies were the backbone of wired networking, and they set the pace for the wireless networking technology. The term "wired" implies a technology that is done via a physical medium, such as cables. The cables in question can be twisted pair, copper wire, or fiber-optic. The wired network technology is noted for its ability to carry a wide range of electrical signals from one end of the network to another.

Mostly in this network type, the T1 line is used for an Internet connection. Other devices that are used include cable modems. The wired network concept is used for sharing a connection among a wide range of devices in the wired network concept. The medium of data transfer for the majority of the wired network are Ethernet cables. These cables are effective for data transfer between personal computers that are connected together.

If the wired network is relatively small, all the computers on the network will be connected to a single router. In larger networks, switches or multiple routers are used for establishing a connection between the devices on the network. One of the switches or cables will connect to a T1 line, a cable modem, or other Internet connection type that has the ability to provide the devices connected to the wired network the desired Internet access. Since the majority of mice and keyboards are currently wireless, it is safe to admit that "wired" can also be used for describing input devices connected to a USB port.

## Types of wired network

The wired network doesn't come in one form but comes in different forms to give users the opportunity to make a choice from the list of available wired network options according to their needs. Consider these few types of wired network:

- **Coaxial cable:** A coaxial cable is a piece of wire used in cable TV connections. The cable is protected by flexible metallic shielding to make it durable.

- **Twisted-pair wire:** These are the standard wires used for phones. A typical example is the wires that connect a local telephone office to home phones.

- **Fiber-optic cable:** These are special wires that use light rather than the conventional electricity used by most cables. The fiber-optic cables are made of glass filaments and are so tiny that they have the same diameter as human hair.

## Advantages of wired network

Sometimes, a wired network may be better than a wireless one due to some of the advantages of wired networking. A good look at the benefits of wired networking will reveal the outstanding advantages of a wired network. Here are some of these benefits:

- **Security:** The physical connection involved in wired networks requires that a cable is physically connected with a device to establish connection with the network. This makes it quite challenging for the network to be accessed without authorization. Someone just passing by your home or office windows doesn't have the opportunity to hack into your wired network. You don't need a wireless access key that can be hacked to access your network since the physically connected device is automatically a part of your network. So, if you are thinking of a very secure and closed network, consider a wired network; it is the best way to go.

- **Reliability:** A wireless network can be affected by the environment. This may have a huge impact on the network's upload and download speeds. This challenge is non-existent with a wired network. Since a wired network doesn't travel through the air, it is not prone to interference or fluctuations in speed from other devices. Thus, a wired network offers more reliability of use than its wireless counterpart.

- **Ease of use:** The details of the wired network depend on the devices on the network and the computers. However, connecting a laptop or printer with an Ethernet cable is sufficient for the device to be connected to the network. This eliminates the need for scanning around for existing networks in the vicinity, entering security keys, or searching for a strong Wi-Fi signal to connect with. Ultimately, though, the ease of use of this network is determined on the type of equipment your company has and the reach of the network cabling in your company.

- **Distance:** The distance covered by this network is another advantage it has over a wireless network. While the fastest 802.11n Wi-Fi speed can only offer you 250 feet as its maximum range under the most ideal conditions, it may be exposed to interference from some physical obstacles such as floors and walls or be interfered with by other devices. The interference will obviously reduce the distance covered by the network. On the other hand, Ethernet cabling can offer you about 330 feet of high-quality service without losing quality. Thus, if you have a wide area to cover, a wired network will be the best option as it allows you to extend your network further than what a wireless network can offer.

- **Speed:** A wired connection has proved time and time again to be faster than a wireless connection. For instance, if you have to transfer some files among local computers, something you may have to do regularly, you will realize that the speed of transfer over a wired network is better than through a wireless connection. Thus, if you are a business owner, it will be more convenient for your employee to exchange or transfer documents and files at an amazing speed that a wireless connection cannot match. The speed of transfer may lead to a rise in production and eliminate the potential frustration that may arise from slower files and document transfer.

- **Real-time applications:** Unlike wireless connections that find it difficult to handle real-time applications such as video and voice, wired connections are known for their ability to handle these real-time applications without fuss. This is a huge advantage of using this networking option since people now use these real-time applications more than ever. The ability of wired networks to handle them perfectly well is a welcome development.

- **Games:** Wired devices are also the preferred choice of gamers. They prefer wired mice and keyboards to their wireless counterparts due to the lower latency offered by these wired peripherals in addition to the backlit attribute of these wired devices.

## Disadvantages of wired network

Despite the good number of advantages of the wired network, it also has some weaknesses. Consider these few disadvantages of wired network:

1- **Limited distance:** One of the biggest disadvantages of a wired network is limited distance of operation. Access to the network can be limited by distance and the user's location since a physical connection is needed to the network to have access to it.

2- **Convenience:** As a wired network user, you will be concerned about the convenience of using the network. It is imperative that you are always within the vicinity of the network and are always physically connected to it before you can use it. Sometimes, it may be quite inconvenient for you to be physically connected to the network, and that automatically shuts you off from access to the network. You may feel awkward moving around with the connection cables and other networking devices you need to connect to a network and use it.

3-    **Expensive:** Sometimes, setting up a wired network may be quite expensive. When you consider the huge amount of ports and cables needed for wired connection, you may have to cough out a huge sum of money to acquire these. This makes a wired connection to sometimes be very expensive, especially if you want to cover a reasonably large area with the wired connection.

4-    **Not meant for public use:** With wireless connection, you have unlimited and unrestricted access to the Internet. Both at home, in the office, at the airport, or while using a public hotel, Wi-Fi gives you access to the Internet on the go. The same cannot be said about a wired connection. You don't enjoy the luxury of use available for wireless connection users.

5-    **Space:** Products of wired technology use more space than needed by their wireless counterparts. A typical example of such product is a desktop computer. A desktop computer requires cables, wires, and other components for operation, far more than the basic requirements for using a wireless laptop. If the products are to be used in offices, you must also factor in space allocation for employees as well as office furniture. Both will account for a good percentage of the needed space.

6-    **Safety:** Using wired products offers less safety than wireless products. The cables may be damaged, wires may be mislaid, and tripping hazards cannot be overruled. These are issues that are alien to wired products.

7-    **Power:** When using wired products, power challenges must also be considered. There may be power outages during stormy weather while electrical problems can also pose power problems as well. If you are using an "always on" wired technology, the problem becomes more pronounced with more impact than using wireless devices.

These are some of the pros and cons of using this technology. The pros are responsible for the proliferation of wireless technology and devices around the globe. How do the wired technologies fare in comparison with the wireless technologies?

# Chapter 5: The world of IP's

Basic Routing concepts

As you could see, the **MAC** address is **only used** for communication within the local network. For example, it is used when 2 PCs send traffic between each other in the LAN. If they would try to communicate on the Internet, then an **IP address** (and a Router) would be required.

The purpose of a **Router** (figure 5.1 - Cisco 2811 model) is to **connect multiple networks** (e.g.: LAN) into a larger network (often called a WAN - Wide Area Network). Thus, the Router's main purpose is to make a simple decision for every single packet that comes in:

"On what interface should I send this packet? And if I don't know where to send it, I'll drop it. "

Figure 5.1

By knowing multiple network locations, a Router can send the traffic from one network to the other. This process of moving the traffic forward, towards its destinations, is known as **routing**.

**ATTENTION!** By default, a **Router** only **knows its Directly Connected** networks. It does not know how to send packets further. This is where we, the administrators, come in. We'll have to tell the Router on which way to go in order to reach the destination.

When a Router boots up, it **first learns** about its **directly connected networks** (those starting with C in Figure 5.2). In the figure 5.2, you can see the routing table of a Cisco Router, which contains the directly connected networks (C) and the IP address of R1 on those interfaces (L).

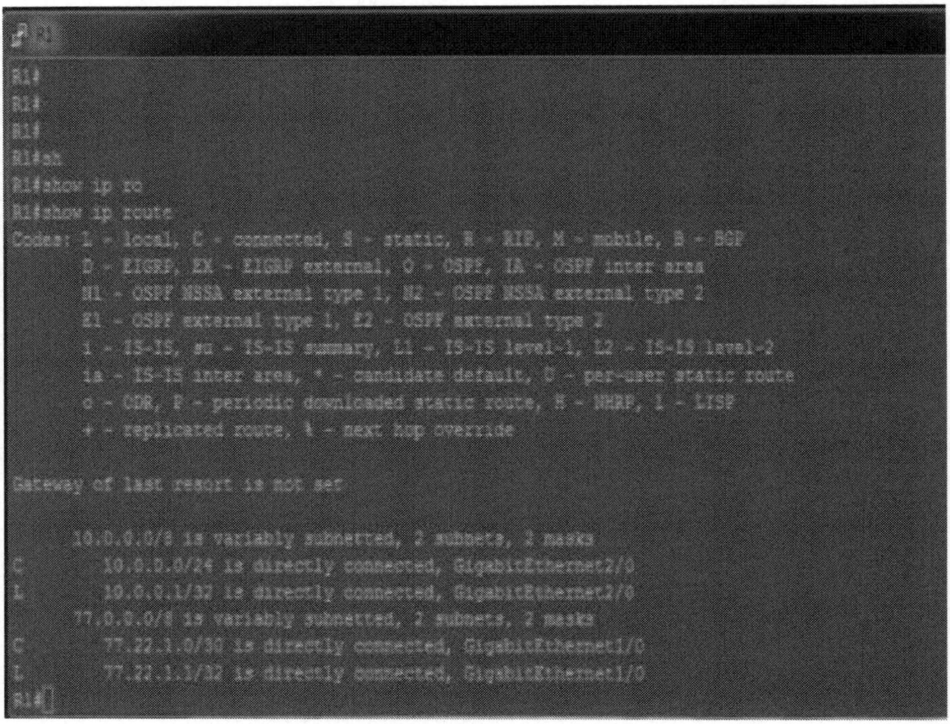

```
R1#
R1#
R1#
R1#sh
R1#show ip ro
R1#show ip route
Codes: L - local, C - connected, S - static, R - RIP, M - mobile, B - BGP
       D - EIGRP, EX - EIGRP external, O - OSPF, IA - OSPF inter area
       N1 - OSPF NSSA external type 1, N2 - OSPF NSSA external type 2
       E1 - OSPF external type 1, E2 - OSPF external type 2
       i - IS-IS, su - IS-IS summary, L1 - IS-IS level-1, L2 - IS-IS level-2
       ia - IS-IS inter area, * - candidate default, U - per-user static route
       o - ODR, P - periodic downloaded static route, H - NHRP, l - LISP
       + - replicated route, % - next hop override

Gateway of last resort is not set

      10.0.0.0/8 is variably subnetted, 2 subnets, 2 masks
C        10.0.0.0/24 is directly connected, GigabitEthernet2/0
L        10.0.0.1/32 is directly connected, GigabitEthernet2/0
      77.0.0.0/8 is variably subnetted, 2 subnets, 2 masks
C        77.22.1.0/30 is directly connected, GigabitEthernet1/0
L        77.22.1.1/32 is directly connected, GigabitEthernet1/0
R1#
```

Figure 5.2

Making the routing process possible, the Router uses the **destination IP address** as a reference point (**"to whom should the traffic be sent?"** - the **destination**) and the source IP address as the **source** (**"from where did the traffic come from?").**

In order to send the traffic (packets) to its destination, the Router needs to know, first of all, the destination. This can be done only if the **Router learns** how to reach that destination, a process that can be achieved by one of 2 ways:

- **Manual** - via Static Routes

- **Dynamic** - via Routing Protocols (RIP, OSPF, EIGRP)

In the following sections, we will start talking about the **IPv4** and **IPv6** protocols (and addresses), then in Chapter 8, we'll move on to the practical side and configuring a Cisco Router in the network simulator Cisco Packet Tracer.

What is IPv4?

The **IPv4 protocol** was developed in the 1980s and it was designed to use **32 bits** of data in order to define an IP address (ex: **192.168.1.1**). As you can see in the example 192.168.1.1, there are 4 fields separated by dots and each field of these 4 can be allocated 8 bits of data:

**8** bits * **4** fields = **32** bits.

Now, let's think a bit about this number of bits, 32. It can tell us something about the maximum number of IP addresses that can be generated: $2 \wedge 32 \sim= $ **4.3 Billion**!

Yeah, you read it well, 4.3 billion IPv4 addresses ... and they would be **all allocated**.

**TIP**: why $2 \wedge 32$? because each bit can be 0 or 1, so if we have 32 bits, we can generate about 4.3 billion unique numbers/addresses.

In 2011, exactly in the summer of that year, **IANA** (**I**nternet **A**ssigned **N**umbers **A**uthority) has allocated the last IPv4 address space. Does that mean we can't connect other devices to the Internet anymore? Not at all. Since then, the Internet has grown a lot. Here's a graph (figure 5.3) that predicts the growth of the

Internet in terms of the connected devices:

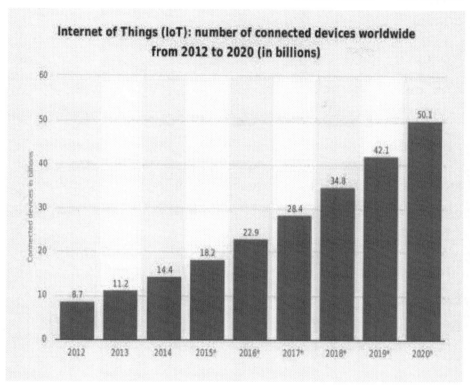

Figure 5.3

**NOTE**: please note that there is a difference between **being allocated** and **being used**. IANA has provided all of its available IP addresses to the Service Providers (ISP) from all around the world, but these addresses are far from being USED by the ISP (or more exactly used by us, the consumers).

As I said earlier, the maximum number of IPv4 addresses is **~4.3 Billion**.

In 2016, it was estimated that the **total number** of **devices connected** to the **Internet** will be around ~**20 billion**, which by far exceeds the IPv4 address number.

Due to this problem, measures have been taken to **slow IPv4 address** allocation by using techniques such as NAT, and also to introduce the concept of **Public and Private IP**. To another extent, far better than NAT is the introduction of the **IPv6 protocol**, which we will discuss a little bit later.

The Structure of an IPv4 Packet

In figure 5.4 you can see the structure (header) of an IPv4 packet

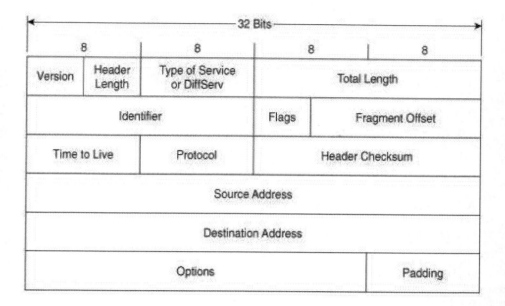

Figure 5.4

Here, we can identify some important components that we'll interact with in many situations, throughout our IT studies/career:

- IP Source Address

- IP Destination Address

- **TTL** (**T**ime **to** **L**ive)

- **ToS** (**T**ype **of** **S**ervice)

- Header Checksum

Now, let's talk about each of these in more detail, and let's start with the IP addresses. I assume that it's clear the fact that in any communication, between 2 devices, we need a **source address** and a **destination address**.

In this case, the two fields (Source & Destination Address) are reserved for the **source IP** address and **destination IP** address.

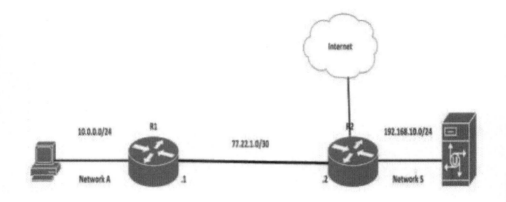

Figure 5.5

For example, in Figure 5.5 you can see the 2 networks: A and S. If the PC from Network A (with the IP 10.0.0.5) wants to communicate with the server (with the IP 192.168.10.8) from network S, then the source address of each packet will be **10.0.0.5** (PC's IP), and the destination address will be **192.168.10.8** (Server's IP).

IPv4 Classes

As I said at the beginning of this chapter, each field (4 in total) of an IP address can have any value between **0 - 255** (8 bits / field, so 256 values, $2 \wedge 8 = 256$). Thus, IP addresses are divided into several classes:

| IP Class | Start IP | End IP | Network Prefix |
|---|---|---|---|
| A | 1.0.0.0 | 127.255.255.255 | 1 - 127 |
| B | 128.0.0.0 | 191.255.255.255 | 128 - 191 |
| C | 192.0.0.0 | 223.255.255.255 | 192 - 223 |
| D | 224.0.0.0 | 239.255.255.255 | 224 - 239 |
| E | 240.0.0.0 | 255.255.255.255 | 240 - 255 |

**Classes A, B and C** are the ones **used in the Internet**, Class D being reserved for Multicast addresses, and Class E being an experimental class that is not being used.

Public IP vs Private IP

**Public IP** addresses, as their name says, are being used to communicate (transit) over the (Public) Internet, and the **Private IP** addresses are used in Local Area Networks (**LANs**) such as our home network or our school's network.

Thus, **Private IP addresses will never reach the Internet**. In order for us to be able to communicate over the Internet, a protocol such as **NAT** (Network Address Translation) will be created with the purpose of **transforming Private IPs into Public IPs**.

Private IP Addresses

In the table below are the ranges of the Private IP addresses out there:

| IP Class | Start IP | IP End | Network Prefix |
|----------|----------|--------|----------------|
| A | 10.0.0.1 | 10.255.255.255 | 10.0.0.0/8 |
| B | 172.16.0.1 | 172.31.255.255 | 172.16.0.0/12 |
| C | 192.168.0.1 | 192.168.255.255 | 192.168.0.0/16 |

NOTE: The rest of the IP addresses not mentioned in this table are PUBLIC!

Thus, we can have a scenario similar to the one in figure 5.6 below (multiple LANs - Network A and S - which contain private IP addresses and public IP addresses for the rest of the networks).

Also, these Private IP addresses (with the help of NAT) improve our **network's security,** making it harder for potential attackers to enter it.

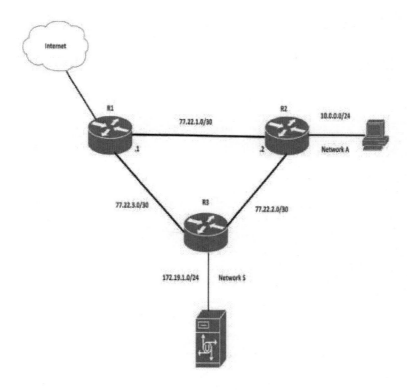

Figure 5.6

3 ways of sending Packets in the Network

Have you ever thought of how end-devices or network devices send the packets in the network? Well, here are the 3 options available out there:

- *Unicast*

- *Multicast*

- *Broadcast*

In the **Unicast mode**, communication between 2 devices is **1 to 1**. This means there is a single source and a single destination. Think of unicast as talking to a friend (you're addressing yourself to only one person).

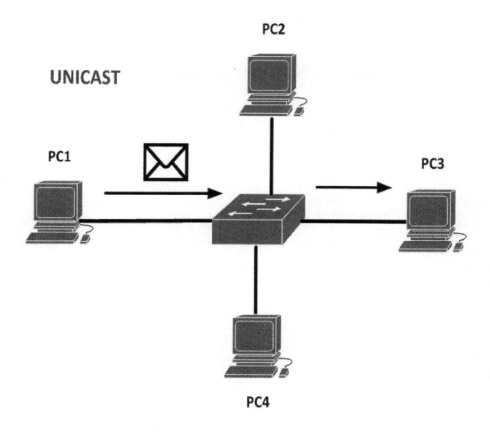

UNICAST

PC2

PC1

PC3

PC4

Figure 5.7

In **Multicast mode**, the communication between devices is **1 to many** (specific group of devices). Imagine that you are in a room with 100 people, and you only have a conversation with a group of 10 people / colleagues (aka specific group). This is multicast.

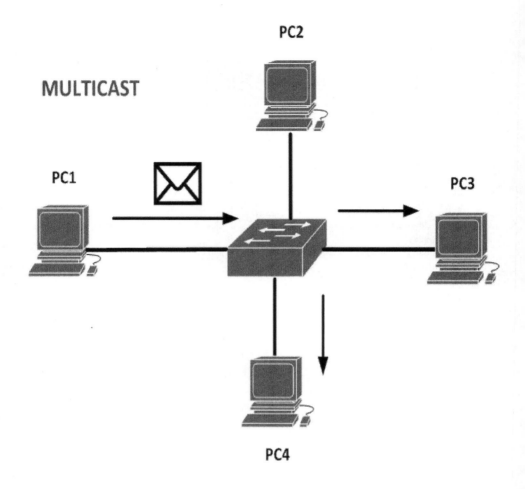

Figure 5.8

In **Broadcast mode**, the communication between devices is **1 to n** (where n represents all devices in the network). **The Broadcast traffic is intended for every device in the network**.

Once again, imagine you are in the same room with 100 people, you are on a stage and you talk to everyone. This is the equivalent of the broadcast.

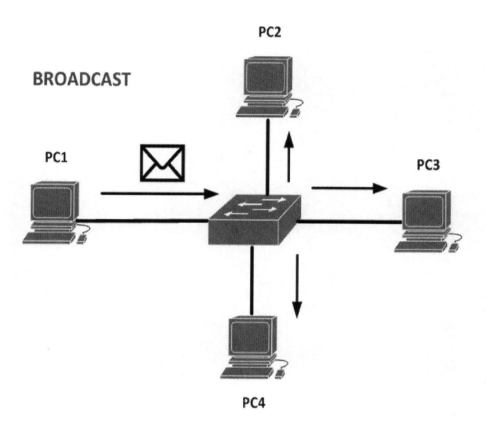

Figure 5.9

Configuring an IP address on Windows 7/8/10

On Windows, when it comes to setting up an IP address, we have 2 options: from the command line, or from the GUI.

First, we'll start by checking our IP address from the command line:

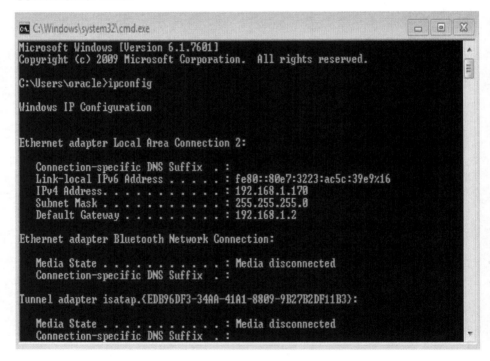

Figure 5.10

The command that's used in figure 5.10 is **>ipconfig** and as you can see, it shows us more information about the Ethernet (LAN), Wi-Fi, Bluetooth adapters. The most important elements shown by the command's output are:

- IPv4 Address

- Network Mask

- Default gateway

- IPv6 Address

All of these elements can be configured in one of 2 ways:

- **Statically** - we'll assign all of the info manually

- **Dynamically** - a protocol (such as DHCP) was configured on a server and assigns dynamically IP addresses, with no human interaction at all.

Ok, now let's see how we can configure on Windows 7 (8.1 or 10), all of the elements mentioned above. In figures 5.11 and 5.12, you'll be able to see how we can do this:

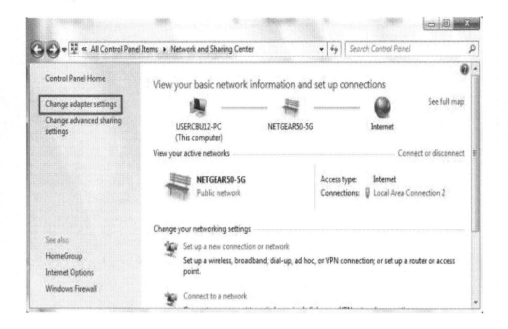

Figure 5.11

A very simple way to configure a **static IP address** is to go to the "**Control Panel -> Network and Sharing Center**" first, followed by "**Change adapter settings**" (or **Network and Internet -> Network Connections**). Now you'll reach a window similar to the one shown in the figure 5.12:

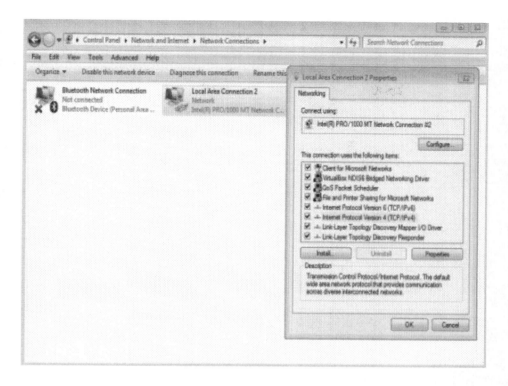

Figure 5.12

Here, we are looking for the "**Local Area Connection 2**" (in your case might be a similar name), and **right click** on it, followed by **"Properties"**. A new window will open, from which we'll **select IPv4** and then **click on Properties**.

At this point we have reached a similar window to the one in figure 5.13. Here, we can (finally) set **the IP**

**address, the Subnet Mask, Default Gateway and the DNS Server:**

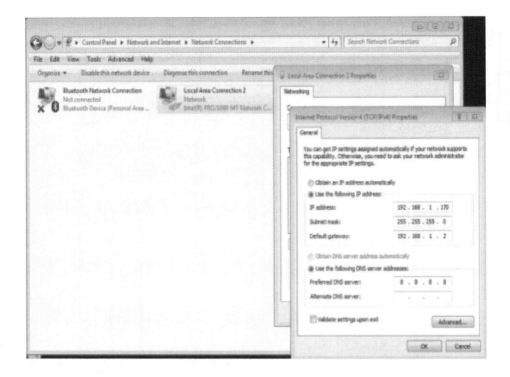

Figure 5.13

Now let's choose, for the sake of this example, a network from which we'll select the other elements required to have access to the Internet. The network's IP address will be 192.168.1.0/24, out of which **192.168.1.170** will be assigned to the PC (Windows 7). The **/24** in decimal mask looks 255.255.255.0 and the

**default gateway** (the Internet-connected Router) will have the IP address of 192.168.1.2.

We also need to set the **DNS** server (the one that helps us with the name resolution: from a domain (ex: google.com) will provide us with its IP address (ex: 216.58.214.227)) of **8.8.8.8**

Now that we're done with all of these settings, we can check our configuration (from CMD) using the following commands:

>**ping   8.8.8.8**              //checks the Internet connection (actually to 8.8.8.8, which is a Google's server)

>**ping google.com**        //checks the DNS service **and** the Internet connection

>**nslookup   google.com**        //checks the DNS service

In the next section we'll start talking about the successor of IPv4, the "new" **IPv6** protocol.

What is IPv6?

Today, there are more than 20 Billion devices connected to the Internet all around the world, and the number keeps getting bigger and bigger, as days pass by. This is a major problem, especially for ISPs (Internet Service Providers), because it exceeds by far the number of 4.3 Billion, which IPv4 was providing.

So here comes the need for a better, much larger protocol, which is known as IPv6. IPv6 is a new addressing (identification) protocol that introduces a new address format (in hexadecimal) and a much, **much larger addressing space**.

**IPv6 is 128 bits long** (that means we have $2 \wedge 128$ addresses available), which is an infinitely large space when compared to IPv4 (that is only 32 bits long). Besides, these features IPv6 has will streamline the communication process of devices in the Internet, making everything faster and more secure.

**WolframAlpha** computational knowledge engine.

2^128                                                                    ☆ 🔖

⊞ ⊞ ⊞ ❀                              ⠿ Web Apps    ☰ Examples   ⤨ Random

Input:
$2^{128}$

Open code 🔗

Result:
340 282 366 920 938 463 463 374 607 431 768 211 456

Scientific notation:
$3.40282366920938463463374607431768211456 \times 10^{38}$

🔗

Number names:                                                      Full name

340 undecillion ...

340 billion billion billion billion ...

Number length:

39 decimal digits

🔗

Figure 5.14

Here are a few examples of IPv6 addresses:

- 2001:DB8:85A3:8D45:119:8C2A:370:734B /64

- **FE80::C001:37FF:FE6C:0/64**

95

- **2001::1/128**

As you can see, IPv6 addresses are represented in the **hexadecimal format** (it includes the **digits 0-9** and **letters A-F**). An IPv6 address is comprised of up to **8 fields** and a network mask (indicating how large the network is - the number of addresses).

Notes: Each IPv6 address field is separated by ":", but there can be a few exceptions:

**2002:ABCD:1234:BBBA:0000:0000:0000:0001/64** can also be written in the following ways:

a) 2002:ABCD:1234:BBBA**:0:0:0:**1/64

b) 2002:ABCD:1234:BBBA**::**1/64

If we want to **reduce** a whole **integer of 0s**, we will simplify it by "::". **ATTENTION** ! "::" can be **used** only **once**.

In Figure 5.15 below, you can see an IPv6 address (command **>ipconfig**) from CMD that begins with the notation of **FE80**:...

This **IPv6 address** is a **special** one, in the sense that it can only be used in the local area network (**LAN**) to communicate with other devices.

This type of address is known as **Local Link** and is generated automatically (another important feature of IPv6 - address auto-configuration).

Figure 5.15

# Chapter 6: History of Internet

The computer networking industry has continued to impact people's lives and businesses over the years. Almost all the sectors of the human economy have been impacted either directly or indirectly by networking, and it will continue to have much influence in the future as well. What started out as a group of computers designed to send commands to each other has gradually become a sector covering the cloud, Wi-Fi, Internet of Things, Network Attached Storage, and other technologies. However, what's the origin of this highly influential technology?

## *1940*

One of the earliest foundations of computer networking was laid by George Stibitz in 1940. Recognized as one of the fathers of the modern digital computer, George used a teletype — an electromechanical typewriter for sending and receiving typed messages — to send a series of commands to the New York-based Complex

Number Computer over telegraph lines. This was the first remote use of computing machine.

## The 1950s

In the late 1950s, The Semi-Automatic Ground Environment, a military radar system was created. It was one of the early networks of computers that were connected together to make communication between them possible. It lays the foundation for today's wireless communication technology, a powerful influence on the industry.

### *1960*

In 1960, IBM received an order from the American Airlines to implement the reservation system known as SABRE (Semi-Automatic Business Research Environment). The implementation of the commercial airline reservation system led to the birth of the online transaction process. By using telephone lines, SABRE was able to link some 22,000 terminals to a pair of IBM 7090 computers across 65 cities. This enabled the system to make fast delivery of data on a flight in a record less than three seconds. Before the implementation of this system, American Airline manually handled its flight bookings through a team of eight operators. The team was saddled with the responsibility of sorting through a rotating file filled up with cards for each flight. Thus, by using the SABRE system, online transactions were gradually introduced into computer networking.

## 1962

The Intergalactic Computer Network was created by J.C.R. Licklider in 1962. Hired by the Advanced Research Projects Agency (ARPA), Licklider developed a working group that connected the teletypewriter and other output systems to computers. the Intergalactic Computer Network was an impressive concept that gave room for programs and data stored in each computer to be open for accessing by users from any part of the world through computers that are connected to the network.

## 1964

The Dartmouth Time Sharing System was developed in 1964 for the use of distributers of large computer systems. While that was on-going, the Massachusetts Institute of Technology was busy cooking up another important technology. The General Electric and Bell Labs-sponsored research group was able to route telephone connections as well as manage the connection via computer.

## *1965*

The Wide Area Network was created by Lawrence G. Roberts and Thomas Marill in 1965. The WAN cleared the way for the Advanced Research Projects Agency Network (ARPANET), one of the greatest contributors to modern day computer networking. Roberts later became the program manager at ARPANET and continued his contributions to the realization of computer networking. In another development, Western Electric introduced the first computer-controlled telephone switch. Since then, different types of switches have contributed their little quota to the development of the computer networking industry.

## 1972

The deployment of commercial services that were using X.25 took place this year. In addition, this new invention was later used as the backbone behind the expansion of the TCP/IP networks.

## The 1980s

The 1980s saw the introduction of ARPANET into the computing world. This technology was expanded in the early 1980s. For instance, The Internet protocol suite, the TCP/IP suite, was introduced as the adopted networking protocol to be used on the ARPANET, and it was the first network to implement it. ARPANET is also one of the earliest packet switching networks and was funded at its early stage by ARPA an arm of the United States Department of Defense.

The early 1980s also witnessed the establishment of several centers for supercomputing, funded by NSF. These centers were built at many universities and provided interconnectivity a couple of years later in 1986 with another project, the NSFNET project. This project also gave some supercomputer sites in the US network access for education and research organizations. In the late 1980s, Internet service providers (ISPs) were gradually introduced into the sector. The ISP is an organization that allows people to gain access to, participate in, or use the Internet. ISPs can be organized into different forms such as non-profit, community-owned, commercial, or privately-owned. Some of the services provided by ISPs are Internet transit, Internet access, web hosting, domain name registration, Usenet service, web hosting, and collocation.

## *1991*

1991 witnessed the creation of home broadband such as ADSL and others in that category. The high-speed system is used at home for linking computers to the Internet. The system uses a DSL or a satellite modem connected to the Internet Service Provider and a cable for operation. A home broadband network is an equally fast internal network used at home for connecting the computers at home together. This home network relies on wireless Wi-Fi technologies and wired Ethernet for operation, two technologies that are faster than most Internet connections' broadband speeds.

## 1996

1996 saw the invention of the 56k modem by Dr. Brent Townshend. The 56k modem allows users with telephone lines to enjoy a faster connection with this new modem. This was a welcome development because it gives Internet users the opportunity to use the Internet without wasting their time and data. It also paved the way for the invention of other technologies that make Internet usage faster, better, and easier.

## The 2000s

This technology was primarily designed for Internet users who do more frequent data downloading than data uploading. Some of its awesome characteristics are high-speed service, voice and data support, "always on," and incredible performance.

## 2001

This year witnessed a surge in the use of home broadband as it entered mainstream usage in that year.

As a result, it embarked on an impressive growth that made it to be faster than Internet dial-up services.

## 2005

In 2005, an online personal cloud content management and file sharing service was launched by Box. The services were launched for business owners to manage their businesses effectively. A year later, Amazon Web Services joined the industry with its cloud storage service. This innovation was widely accepted and gained widespread recognition due to its ability to provide the necessary storage facilities to Pinterest, Dropbox, and other emerging services, allowing Internet users to store their personal information and other resources in the cloud (Internet) where their security is better guaranteed than if such pieces of sensitive information are only stored on personal computers.

## 2011

Another milestone was reached in 2011 with the introduction of the fiber-optic broadband to the computer networking community. Since it came with DOCSIS standards, it offered a broadband speed of

100Mbps. The implication is that end users must acquire better routers that are powerful enough to match the speed of this amazing broadband. The combination of this fast broadband and an equally powerful router will give a user a top-notch networking delivery.

## *2014*

Three years after the introduction of the fiber-optic broadband with its amazing speed, a new Wi-Fi standard launched. The 802.11ac outperformed its predecessor, the 802.11n standard with a fast speed of over 2Gbps in comparison with the latter's 450Mbps. Well, this new standard is not all about speed; it also offered improved signal coverage over its predecessor as well.

# Chapter 7: Introduction to protocols

Network protocols are "formal standards and policies comprised of rules, procedures and formats that define communication between two or more devices over a network." These protocols are responsible for governing the end-to-end process of secure, timely, and managed network communication or data. Included in a network protocol are the requirements, processes, and constraints associated with initiating a communication between servers, computers, routers, and other devices. The protocol is also responsible for ensuring that the initiated conversation is completed.

Both the sender and the receiver must install the protocol to ensure that data/network communication can take place between them. Protocols are used in networking to serve as a medium through which a network can be accessed with the right credentials. The essence is to ensure the feasibility of the connection as well as an identifier for whatever devices within a network. Network protocols are divided into several broad types. This includes:

## Internet Protocols

The Internet Protocol ranks among the most popular and widely used network protocols. In addition to the Internet Protocol, other members of this family are UDP, TCP, HTTP, and FTP. All these protocols are integrated with the Internet Protocol to offer additional capabilities to the users.

## Transmission Control Protocol (TCP)

The Transmission Control Protocol is one of the best protocols and is used for transmitting data over networks. This protocol is designed to ensure reliable data transmission in networks. By default, TCP works with Internet Protocol (IP) to form a dual protocol known as TCP/IP. If you check your computer's settings, you will see the TCP/IP term in it. It is also available in portable devices and smartphones if you check the settings. As a protocol, the TCP is a set of procedures and rules that determines how data transmission is done to ensure that people all over the world transfer data in the same way regardless of the software used, the location of the people, or the hardware used for the data transmission.

On the other hand, the IP handles how data packets are addressed and forwarded from its source to the destination leaving the reliability of the data transmission for the TCP to handle. The TCP's primary responsibility is to control how data is transferred to ensure its reliability. Data is usually transmitted in packets on the Internet. These packets are units of data independently sent on the network. Once data reaches its destination, it is reassembled to the original format so that the receiver will receive the original data. Data transmission is done in layers on a network. Each of the protocols on a layer will discharge its duties complementary to what other protocols on the layer are doing. The set of layers is generally known as a protocol stack.

In the stack, the IP and TCP work together, one above the other to discharge their duties satisfactorily. For instance, when you have HTTP-TCP-IP-Wi-Fi in a stack, it simply means that the HTTP protocol has the responsibility of getting the web page in HTML format. The transmission will be handled by the TCP while the IP handles the channeling on the Internet. Lastly, the Wi-Fi is responsible for how it is transferred on the local area network. In the scenario, you can see that TCP performs its duty of ensuring that the reliability of the transmitted data is not lost during transmission. Thus, the data transmission meets the basic requirements for data to be considered reliable. The requirements are:

- **Complete delivery:** All the packets must be delivered to the destination as a complete entity without losing a packet in transit. For instance, how will you feel if your instant messages or email is delivered to you with some sentences or words missing? It is the responsibility of TCP to ensure that such a disaster never happens.

- **Data quality is guaranteed:** Regardless of how the data is delayed in transit, its quality should not be compromised. While having a VoIP call, you obviously won't appreciate inconsistent transmission.

- **Orderliness:** When the packets are reassembled after getting to their destination, they shouldn't be rearranged haphazardly. Rather, they should be reassembled in order to ensure that the receiver gets nothing but the original data sent.

Imagine if your application letter is rearranged randomly before it is submitted to your prospective employer. Nobody would ever pray for such an

111

unfortunate incident, and TCP also ensures that such a misfortune is averted by ensuring that transmitted data are arranged properly before delivery.

## User Datagram Protocol

This protocol came into existence in 1980 when network protocol was still a novelty. The protocol is a transport layer protocol designed to be used for client/server network applications. The OSI protocol derives is also based on Internet Protocol and remains the best alternative to the more popular TCP. The protocol also forms a dual partnership with IP, forming the UDP/IP. It is mostly used for computer games and video conferencing applications where real-time performance is needed. To give its users value for their money and trust in the protocol, it only allows packets to be dropped individually. More so, UDP packets are not rearranged in order but are delivered in a different order as determined by the application.

In comparison with the TCP, the UDP gives room for less delays and data overhead. Less bandwidth is also required since there is no error-checking in the protocol, and the data will be delivered regardless of its nature.

112

UDP is the ideal protocol for applications where less latency is needed for operation. Such applications include video chatting, online gaming, or voice transmissions. In such situation, there may be a loss of packets, but the little latency delay associated with this protocol ensures that there will only be an insignificant quality loss.

While using the protocol for online gaming, the game will continue despite a momentary loss of connection or if there is a drop of packet. Sometimes, error correction may be a part of the problem. If this occurs, there will be time loss in the connection because the packet will be striving to start from where the connection broke to make up for whatever errors in the connection. This is unnecessary with live streaming and live video games.

UDP also has some port numbers. These numbers make it possible for a wide range of applications to have channels dedicated to data just as TCP also has. Note that UDP port headers have numbers from 0 to 65535 because the headers are two bytes long.

## Hypertext Transfer Protocol

Hypertext Transfer Protocol is one of the most important protocols and is responsible for providing the network protocol standard used by servers and web browsers for communication. The HTTP shares some similarities with FTP because a client program uses the protocol for requesting files from a remote server. HTTP is a web browser that approaches a web server and makes requests for HTML files. The requested files are then displayed with images, text, hyperlinks, etc. in the browser.

Once it makes the request, the HTTP connection drops automatically. This is quite different from the mode of operation of other protocols such as FTP and makes the HTTP to be referred to as a "stateless system." The implication is that once the server responds to your browser's request, the connection between your browser and the server will immediately close. HTTP uses the following three different message types:

- **HTTP GET:** When messages are sent to a server, they contain just the Uniform Resource Locator (URL). Some optional data parameters

114

or zero may be added to the end of the URL. The optional data is processed by the server and then returns the result of the processing to the browser. In most cases, the result of the request can be the element of a web page or a web page.

- **HTTP POST:** The post option allows optional data parameters to be placed in the requested message's body rather than adding the optional data parameters to the end of the Uniform Resource Locator (URL).

- **HTTP HEAD:** This option shares the same mode of operation with the GET option. Rather than reply with the URL's full contents, the server only sends the header information back to the web browser. The header information is usually found in the HTML section. To initiate communication with the with an HTTP server, the browser will first make the TCP be connected to the server. By default, port 80 is dedicated to web sessions by the server although it sometimes allows some ports such as 8080 for the same purpose. When a user visits a web page, he or she triggers the receiving or sending of HTTP messages after the server has established a session. Sometimes, a message transmitted over this protocol may fail to reach its destination and be delivered. This can be caused by several factors such as:

- Malfunction of the web server or the web browser

- *User error*

- Temporary network problems

Whenever these problems arise, the protocol immediately springs to action and finds out the major cause of the failure. It then reports its findings as an error code to the browser known as HTTP status line/code. An error is usually preceded by a certain number that reveals the type of error it is.

## File Transfer Protocol

This protocol's name has really given an idea of what it does. The protocol allows users to use network protocol derived from the Internet Protocol for transferring copies of files between files. The process of copying files by using this technology is also referred to as FTP. FTP was designed to make file sharing on TCP/IP possible. The protocol was also designed to support file sharing on some older networks as well. The protocol makes use of the client-server communication model.

File transfer with FTP is pretty easy. As a user, you only need to run an FTP client program from where you initiate a communication to another computer that runs the FTP server software, although from a remote place. When the connection is established, you can choose to either receive or send copies of files as a group or singly. There is a variation of this protocol known as the Trivial File Transfer Protocol (TFTP). This protocol was designed for a purpose: to offer support for low-end computers. This protocol also offers a similar support offered by FTP, but the protocol is simpler and its set of commands are common to most file transfer operations.

The port commonly used by this protocol is TCP port 21. It uses this port for listening for incoming connection requests made by FTP clients. The server also uses port

21 for controlling the connection and then opens another port to be used exclusively for file data transfer only.

## Wireless Network Protocols

Wireless Network Protocols refer to a set of protocols used extensively for wireless operations. Although many people consider Wi-Fi to be synonymous with wireless networking, the network isn't strictly for Wi-Fi but supports a long list of protocols. There is no perfect protocol that can meet people's different wireless needs. Some protocols are optimized for battery conservation on mobile devices while a good number of protocols are equally designed for high speed, longer-distance connections and more reliability. Here is a short list of these protocols:

### *LTE*

Before the fourth-generation wireless technology and networking were introduced and adopted by smartphones, mobile phones used different older generation protocols for cellular communication. Some of these protocols are GPRS, HSDPA, and EV-DO. Today, the phone industry and its carriers have invested a small fortune to upgrade the older protocols and cell towers to support the new generation, the fourth generation (4G). 4G was used to standardize a communication protocol generally known as Long Term Evolution (LTE), which became popular in 2010.

Some of the challenges with older protocols include roaming issues and low data rates. On the other hand, the LTE protocol has the capacity to carry in excess of 10 Mbps for each user. However, as a result of high equipment costs and some challenges triggered by government regulations, phone carriers are yet to implement this protocol in many parts of the world. More so, this protocol is not ideal for home use or for local area networks because it was designed for customers living in far, distant places.

## *Wi-Fi*

Wi-Fi is undeniably the best wireless networking technology for public hotspot and home networks. In the 1990s, this technology was used extensively as the hardware for networking used extensively for enabling printers, PCs, and others. It gradually become affordable globally and its data rates improved from a mere 11Mbps to an impressive 54Mbps.

Although this technology can be effective over long distances if operated in a controlled environment, it is ideal for use in commercial buildings, single residential buildings, and outdoor areas within the neighborhood. Today, both LTE and Wi-Fi are supported by mobile devices so they can offer more flexibility to the users in whatever networks they are using.

## *Bluetooth*

Bluetooth is another protocol that has been available for ages. This technology was created for synchronizing data between phones and other battery-powered devices. Bluetooth uses more power than Wi-Fi and a good number of other wireless protocols. The Bluetooth connection is only effective within 30 feet and can be used with low data rates of between 1 and 2Mbps. On some new devices, Bluetooth has been completely replaced with Wi-Fi. However, some phones still have both the Bluetooth and Wi-Fi features.

## 60GHz Protocols

Streaming video data is currently one of the activities performed most on computer networks. Tons of wireless protocols have been built to run on the 60GHz frequencies. The goal is to support streaming and other usages where a huge amount of network bandwidth is required. In the 2000s, two distinct standards, WiGig and WirelessHD were created. Both of these standards use the 60GHz technology to support wireless connections that use high bandwidth. While the former standard offers just a small bandwidth of between 1 and 7Gbps, the latter offers an impressive bandwidth between 10 and 28Gbps. Although Wi-Fi networks can be used for basic video streaming, high data rates are needed for top-notch high-definition video streaming. Such high data rates are offered by these protocols.

## Network Routing Protocols

Routing protocols are not ordinary protocols you can find anywhere. This protocol is a special-purpose protocol that is specifically designed for network routers on the Internet. This protocol can easily manage the routes between destinations and sources of network messages, identify other routers, and make important and effective routing decisions. Over the years, scores of network protocols have been designed and created to give maximum support to communication between electronic devices and between computers. Routing protocols are special network protocols that make communication between computer routers possible. Thus, the routers can easily exchange traffic between the routers' respective networks.

Each routing protocol is known to perform these basic functions:

- **Discovery:** It must identify all the existing routers on the network.

- **Route management:** It must keep a tab on the possible destinations and data that describe the pathway of the destinations.

- **Path determination:** It must decide in advance where each network message should be sent.

There are some routing protocols known as the link state protocols. These protocols give a router the permission to build a map of the network links in a specific region and equally track the region. Some others known as distance vector protocols also allow routers to use the limited information it has about the network area. Some routing protocols and their functions are discussed below.

## RIP

The Routing Information Protocol (RIP) was created by some researchers to be used on small- or medium-sized internal networks. It is a dynamic protocol generally used for finding the best route for sending messages over a network. It uses the hop count/routing metric algorithm to determine the shortest path the message can take from the sender to the receiver. This allows data to be swiftly delivered to the destination at high speed. These networks established a connection to the Internet. The protocol can route up to 15 hop messages across networks.

RIP plays a significant role in providing the best and shortest path that a data can take from one node to another. The hop simply refers to the step taken towards the nearest device, which can be a computer, router, or any other device on the network. Once the hop's length has been determined, the RIP will store this information in a routing table where it will be kept for future use.

A RIP router has a routing table where all the networks or destinations it can reach and the distances to the destinations are kept in a list. It then uses a special algorithm, the distance vector algorithm, to identify the best route it can put a packet on and successfully reach its destination. If RIP receives an update about a specific route and realizes that the distance is shorter, it will immediately update the table entry with the shorter path's next hop address as well as the length. On the other hand, if the new path will take more time, it will wait until other updates reflect the shorter path or not. If they do, it will automatically update its table entry if it realizes that the new path is stable.

With the RIP, each router will forward its routing table to other routers it is directly connected to, known as neighbors. The neighbor will also do the same and pass their routing tables to their nearest neighbors until all the existing RIP hosts in the network have the same routing table and routing path, commonly referred to as convergence.

Whenever a network connection is disconnected or a router crashes, the network will be immediately informed because the router will stop sending updates to the nearest routers. It may also stop receiving and sending updates along the disconnected connection. If a route in the routing table is not updated for 180 seconds or six successive update cycles, the route will be immediately dropped by a RIP router and immediately inform the other members of the network as it updates the network about the problem and immediately starts the re-converging process on another network topology. RIP is a protocol used in both wide and local area networks. The protocol is considered by many users as very easy to configure and implement. The traditional RIP only supported the IPv4 networks, while the newer RIPng supports IPv6 also. RIP uses either the 521 (RIPng) or UDP ports 520 for communication.

## *OSPF*

The Open Shortest Path First addresses some limitations such as:

- RIP's inability to efficiently organize networks into a hierarchy that make performance and manageability possible on big internal networks

- RIP's 15 hop count restriction

- The generation of spikes of network traffic triggered by resending full router tables repeatedly at prescheduled intervals

This protocol is an open public standard that has been widely adopted by a good number of industry vendors. Routers with OSPF connections can discover a network simply by exchanging identification messages with each other. In addition, messages with information about specific routing items are also exchanged, rather than exchanging the entire routing table. Other important network protocols are IS-IS, BGP and EGP, and EIGRP and IGRP.

## Network security protocols

The rapid growth witnessed by the Internet as a business or individual communication channel has led to a growing demand for privacy and security on the Internet. This is needed for the Internet and businesses to thrive because people will not feel comfortable with a system that breaches their privacy and security. Some protocols have been designed over the years to address the privacy and security issues. Some of these network security protocols are:

### Hypertext Transfer Protocol Secure (HTTPS)

HTTP was originally developed for a simple web where dynamic graphics was not an issue. At that time, there was no need for a hard encryption that supported end-to-end transactions. However, with the growing popularity came the need for users to increase the security of their websites, especially entrepreneurs who depend on the Internet for their websites. They also realized the need for more graphics and cryptographic improvements for the Internet to remain the backbone of commerce as promised by the founders. This led to the development of a new protocol that addresses all the issues and ensures the security of the Internet.

HTTPS is an improvement over the traditional HTTP. It provides a platform for the system that enables users to use a computer network for secure communication. This makes it a very popular security protocol. As previously mentioned, the principal motivation for developing the protocol is to ensure that an accessed website is secure while the protection of the integrity and privacy of any data in transit is guaranteed. How popular is this protocol?

Whenever you send sensitive information over this connection, rest assured that the privacy of your information is not compromised. It becomes impossible for an eavesdropper to list in on your information while in transit. This is made possible by HTTPS, a protocol that also ensures that shopping and online banking are made secure. In addition, this protocol also makes your normal web browsing secure by providing an extra layer of privacy for you while browsing. For instance, Google's search engine now adopts the HTTPS connections by default. This implies that nobody can see your search query while using the Google search engine. You also enjoy this privacy while using Wikipedia. However, this was not possible in the past when your privacy and the security of your information could not be guaranteed. Back then, it was possible for other people to see and monitor your searches. Your Internet Service Provider could listen in on your discussion as well.

Although HTTPS was originally designed to offer security for payments, passwords, and other sensitive and confidential data, it has gradually found its way into all other facets of the web. Thus, browsing the web is now more secure than in the past, and your privacy has never been protected as much as the HTTPS protocol does.

## Secure Socket Layer (SSL)

Secure Socket Layer is the undisputed cryptographic protocol designed to provide Internet users security over whatever communications they have over the Internet. The SSL protocol offers users a secure channel for two devices or machines operating over an internal network or the Internet. Whenever a browser attempts to gain access to a website with SSL security, the web server and the browser will establish an SSL connection by using a process commonly referred to as "SSL Handshake." This handshake happens instantaneously and cannot be seen by the user.

It should be brought to your attention that the SSL connection can be set up with three keys: private, public, and session keys. Both the public and private keys are used for encryption. Whatever is encrypted by the private key can be decrypted with the public key and vice versa. Due to the huge amount of processing power required for encryption and decryption, their use is restricted to creating a symmetric session key during the SSL handshake. After making the secure connection, the session key will be used for encrypting all data transmitted over the network.

Over the years, the SSL protocol has been the primary tool for encrypting data as well as securing transmitted data. Whenever a new version of the protocol is released, the version number is always altered to reflect the changes made to the SSL. However, rather than have the SSLv4.0 version, the new protocol was renamed TLSv1.0.

The Transport Layer Security (TLS) protocol makes secure communication available for Internet faxing, e-mail, and other data transfer over the Internet.

# Chapter 8: Virtualization, principal os, server installation, cloud service

The wide areas of applications of wireless networks in modern times are an indication of what the technology will offer in the future. At the moment, wireless networks have simplified a lot of human activities such as communication, business transactions, and other activities. However, the future is brighter than most people can imagine. The modern wireless network will be child's play compared to what the future promises. Let's consider some of the major future development of wireless networks and the potential huge impact they will have on the users. Let me start with Li-Fi.

## Li-Fi

You obviously are aware of the attributes and usefulness of the Wi-Fi wireless technology. As a reminder, this technology is one of the best things that has ever happened to wireless technology. Wi-Fi has really simplified wireless connection and makes it accessible to millions of users around the world.

However, a better version of this wireless network is around the corner. Welcome to the world of Li-Fi. What is Li-Fi?

Li-Fi, Light Fidelity, is the new poster boy of wireless communication technology. This technology carries out data communication through light signals. One of the biggest advantages of this technology is its impressive speed. At the moment, this wireless technology can boast of a speed of 224 gigabits/second. When compared with its predecessor, Wi-Fi, this is a good improvement with tons of benefits for wireless connection users. Professor Harald Hass introduced Li-Fi into the world at a TED Talk in 2011. He had the dream of turning the light bulbs into a better use: wireless routers. Today, he is working towards achieving that dream and may do so in the near future.

To work on his dream, Professor Hass launched Pure Li-Fi after the Talk in 2012. The company was established as a platform for developing Li-Fi product. The company is primarily responsible for developing Li-Fi devices. During the Talk, Professor Hass unveiled his dream.

Since the professor has successfully proved that the light spectrum can be a good medium of data transmission, Li-Fi is then considered as an optical wireless communication medium. Li-Fi communicates data through ultra-violet (visible light) and infra-red waves. The two spectrums have the ability to carry more information than its radio frequency waves counterpart, which explains why Li-Fi is faster than Wi-Fi.

Currently, this technology depends on the light from light-emitting diodes (LEDs) for data communication. Of course, LEDs have a reputation for their low environmental impact, efficiency, and longevity. When this project sees the light of day, you can turn the lights in your office or home into wireless routers. Since LED light bulbs fall into the semiconductor group, the constant electricity the bulb receives can be altered to be dimmer or brighter, depending on your choice.

With the assistance of Visible Light Communication, the current received by the LED bulb can be flicked on and off at an extremely high rate. If you want to access the Li-Fi network, you need a component that can be used for deciphering the light signals as well as a device for light signal detection.

## How does it work?

The Li-Fi network works on a very simple principle. First, a LED light bulb is fed with data and subsequently has a signal processing technology interfaced. The data is pulsed by the LED bulb at a high rate to the photodetector. When the photodetector receives the pulses, it interprets the pulse into an electrical signal. The signal is subsequently converted into binary data, the web content we all use.

Thus, the LED lights are later networked to make data accessible to multiple users through a single LED light or shift from a LED light to another while their access remains unaffected by the move. Li-Fi's high speed and spatial limits can be combined with Wi-Fi and cellular technologies as a connectivity option. The technology is very useful for siphoning off heavy traffic from Wi-Fi and cellular networks. For instance, this technology can be made available in sports stadiums, shopping malls, and other densely populated areas to allow users to consume live streaming, videos, and other content-rich media. When people are using Li-Fi, the capacities of Wi-Fi and cellular networks in the area will be freed up. Naturally, uplinks don't use much capacity like the downlinks with its network-straining capability.

One of the biggest challenges that experts are facing about the Internet of Things (IoT) revolution is how to find the huge capacity needed to handle the data. Well, Li-Fi has come to the rescue. It has proven to be an efficient, viable, and secure solution to that problem. An office, a home, or a factory can leverage the power of the Li-Fi technology for running its high capacity network while the public capacity is not affected in any way.

## Car-to-Car Communication

In the future, a simple wireless technology will take over driving challenges and make our roads safer with reduced accidents. The technology is designed to warn drivers of impending collisions to enable them to prepare in advance to prevent the collision. Known as vehicle-to-vehicle or car-to-car communication, the technology will let cars on the road broadcast their speed, position, brake status, steering-wheel position, and other relevant information to other road users within a couple of meters of the car. This valuable information will be used by the other cars to have a general view of what is going on around them and notify them of potential troubles that even the most cautious and experienced driver may miss. By building anticipation for the potential collision, the driver is best poised to take all necessary precautions to avoid the accident.

At the moment, many cars are equipped with ultrasound or radar technology for detecting vehicles or obstacles. Despite the usefulness of these technologies, their limited sensor range is a big issue to contend with. Cars equipped with the technology can see beyond the nearest obstruction, making it pale in comparison with the car-to-car wireless technology that will soon take over in the nearest future. With over five million accidents recorded in the United States alone every year, resulting in over 30,000 fatal cases, this technology will be a welcome development. At the moment, Japan and Europe are already testing this technology. It is a matter of time before other countries embrace this amazing wireless and life-saving technology.

## The Internet of Things

When people hear the term, Internet of Things, different ideas are formed. Thus, the concept is shrouded in confusion and mystery as it means different things to people from different walks of life.

IoT also comprises micro-electromechanical (MEMS) systems. When MEMS are embedded into an object, it allows you to communicate and interact effectively with the environment. The objects that can be used include controllers in oil refineries and humans with implanted medical devices. Thus, regardless of the numerous definitions of the concept, it is estimated that tens of billions of devices will enjoy Internet connection by 2020. To realize this vision, much is dependent on wireless technology. What happens to the connected billions of devices?

The connected devices have the capacity to generate information and data that Internet users from all walks of life can access regardless of their places of residence.

Therefore, businesses, governments, and individuals are allowed to use the information for making real-time data-driven decisions. In the future, the IoT has tons of areas of applications that will be explored as the technology fully matures. Let's take a look into some of the practical uses of this wireless technology in the future.

## More cities will become smart

At the moment, the IoT wireless technology is embraced mostly by homeowners. This trend is expected to continue in the future, although more cities are expected to adopt this technology. Then, companies and cities will turn to the wireless technology to save time and money in addition to becoming more efficient. The adoption of the technology means that cities can be automated and remotely managed. Useful data can also be collected through video camera surveillance systems, visitor kiosks, taxis, and even bike rental stations.

## Artificial intelligent will become the real "thing"

Thermostats, home hubs, lighting systems, and others will collect data on your pattern of usage and habits. The voice-controlled devices in your home will record whatever you tell them and store the recordings in the cloud. The data collection has a goal: facilitate machine learning.

Machine learning is an integral part of artificial learning because it is designed to help computers "learn" without being programmed for specific uses. The computers are designed to pay attention to whatever information they collect and use the information to learn. In the future, the machines can really learn your preferences through series of data collection and adjust themselves to meet your preferences.

## Routers will become more "smarter" and secure

Routers are mostly used in homes and are vulnerable to attacks because users can't install security software on them. The craze for the adoption of IoT in the consumer market has placed the necessity on manufacturers to make their products available in the market as soon as possible. The impact is that sometimes these manufacturers pay little or no attention to security in their bid to hit the market before their competitors. The home router becomes handy here.

As previously discussed, the router serves as the Internet's entry point into your home. It is true that the connected devices have no way of self-protection, but the router can provide entry point protection. Although the current routers provide some protection through firewalls, password protection, and the ability to be configured to grant access to some selected devices, they are still prone to attacks because they don't have security software installed on them. Thus, malware can still find a way around the security measures and gain access to a network.

Currently, attackers are focusing on effective ways they can exploit the vulnerabilities in IoT devices. In the future, routers will come fully equipped with built-in security software programs that are more effective at shutting off potential intruders than what the current security measure can offer.

## Wearables will remain a niche

It is estimated that by the end of 2018, over 12 million wearables will be sold in the US alone due to the increased adoption of Google Assistant and Amazon Alexa in more devices. The hype surrounding these devices has provided marketers with a new way of dealing with customers. It is expected that the manufacturers and marketers of these devices will not rest on their oars but will build more of these wearables in the future to meet the growing needs for these efficient wireless technologies that have wormed their ways into the hearts of millions of users from all walks of life.

## Cloud computing

Many people have heard this phrase, but only a handful of people understand what cloud computing really means. This simply means that you can store and access data over the Internet, rather than on your computer's hard drive. Thus, the cloud is nothing but a metaphor for the Internet. To give you an idea of how cloud computing works, I will give you two typical examples of cloud computing that billions of people are using:

- **Apple iCloud:** This cloud service is offered by Apple. It is primarily used for online backup and storage. You can also use the cloud service for synchronizing your contacts, mail, calendar, and others. Whatever data you need is at your fingertips on your Mac OS, iOS, or Windows device, although Windows users must install the iCloud control panel to use this tool. In addition to all these services, iCloud is also a very important tool for iPhone users. Its "Find My iPhone" feature allows iPhone users to locate their handset when it goes missing.

- **Google Drive:** This is the complete cloud computing service. Google Drive is designed to work with cloud apps such as Google Sheets, Google Docs, and Google Slides. The use of this cloud computing service is not limited to desktop computer users but is also available for smartphone and iPad users. Separate apps are available for Sheets and Docs as well. In a nutshell, most of the services offered by Google is cloud computing such as Google Calendar, Gmail, and Google Maps. Today, cloud computing has served as the platform where many people have put their skills to use. It has also served as the business companion of many entrepreneurs. Some of what you can do with cloud computing are:

- Store your data, back it up, or recover it through cloud.

- Create new services and apps.

- Host blogs and websites.

- Stream video and audio.

- Create and deliver software.

- Data analysis for patterns and predictions.

Cloud computing offers some benefits that make it a very important technology both now and in the future. A couple of its numerous benefits are:

- **Cost effective:** With cloud computing, you have to think less about buying software and hardware, a very expensive thing. You also don't have to bother yourself with setting up and running datacenters and spending a huge sum of money on round-the-clock electricity, racks of servers, and IT experts that will manage the infrastructure. This saves you a huge amount of money.

- **Speed:** Speed is another benefit you can enjoy from using cloud computing. Whatever computing resources you need will be delivered to you within a couple of minutes. You only need a few mouse clicks to access the services. This will give your business the desired flexibility while the pressure of capacity planning will be taken off you.

- **Performance:** A global network of datacenters is used for running cloud computing services; these datacenters are upgraded regularly by using the latest computing hardware that offers speed and efficiency. Thus, you have access to better resources rather than what a single corporate datacenter can ever offer you. It also offers greater economies of scale and reduced network latency.

- **Reliability:** Disaster recovery, data backup, and other related services are less expensive and easier through data computing. This is because the technology allows data to be mirrored.

Many people, including inventors and technology enthusiasts, are optimistic about the future of wireless technology. The availability of the needed resources and the increasing demand for more wireless devices ensure that inventors will still feed humanity with more technologies that will make life easier and better in the future.

# Chapter 9: Basic cisco and ccna command and requirements

Cisco Packet Tracer is a simulation program that provides you with the option to learn and experiment with various networks and questions. It is a crucial part of computer networking learning experience. Packet tracers provide simulation, authoring, visualizing, and assessment.

A Cisco project about creating a network using Cisco packet tracer is the best way to understand how Cisco 1200 access points work. Three enterprises namely Enterprise 1, Enterprise 2, and Enterprise 3 are connected to the same network through a cloud. Each enterprise has five routers linked together. The network is built using subnets, ten routers, and subnet masks. The steps that are used to create a network using Cisco packet tracer are:

- Open the Network Topology

After opening the network topology on the Cisco Packet Tracer, gain access to the network and identify the components of the network connection such as subnet masks, servers, and routers.

- Cabling

Connect the cables correctly after accessing the cable's section. A proper connection is required to ensure connectivity among the devices present in the network.

- Configuring of IP addresses

By the help of the network address table, set the Internet Protocol addresses on all devices present on the connection or network. This is achieved by accessing the desktop on every device and determining the Internet Protocol address on the configuration section.

- Configure the IP addresses on other devices and routers

After choosing the correct Internet Protocol addresses for the end devices, do the same for routers, by the use of the address table. Do this carefully because there is no desktop on the routers. You can access the installation panel on all devices in the following ways:

i) Configure the Internet Protocol addresses for the router by the help of the address table.

ii) Use a cable from any device connected to the network and link it to the device you intend to configure. You may access the platform terminal on the device to choose the right Internet Protocol addresses.

Configuring the default gateway

The default gateway has to be configured. The default gateway can be found in the addressing table if it has been provided or on the topology of the network.

**Test**

You can test the connection by accessing the command prompt on the computers or devices and ping the Internet Protocol address on which the network is operating. If you receive a response, it merely means that the network was well-configured.

Distance Vector Algorithm

It is an algorithm that is used for routing purposes in computer networking. The terminology **distance vector** means that routes are advertised as vectors of direction and distance. Distance is determined in metric units such as a hop count. **Direction** means the exit interface or the next-hop router. A router using a distance vector protocol for routing doesn't know the exact direction to a destination network. However, the router is fully aware of: the interface to which packets should be relayed and how far it is to the destination network.

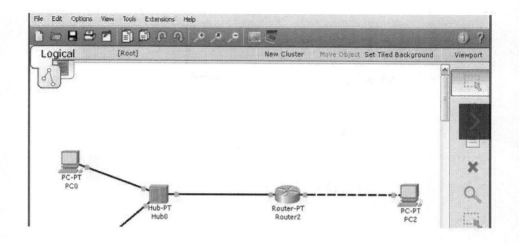

The diagram below shows a Cisco packet tracer:

### Security architecture

- **Define security**

- **Authentication and access control**

- **Encryption benefits**

Logical Wireless Network Architecture

The logical architecture of a computer network is the structure of protocols and standards that establish connections among nodes or devices thereby controlling the flow and routing of information among these devices. Logical connections operate entirely over physical links. Physical and logical architectures not only rely on one another but also have a high chance of independence. The physical architecture can be modified without modifying the logical architecture. The physical network has the capability of supporting various protocols and standards.

Planning a wireless local area connection installation is an activity that cuts across numerous dissimilar disciplines. Wireless local connections deployment can be done perfectly by enhancing network architecture. Wireless connections also have an additional variable called mobility that must be taken seriously.

How do the characteristics of wireless area connections or networks affect the topology of the network? Apart from the 802.11 compatible devices, what other end devices are required to make a network functional? How can you construct a logical network to ensure maximum mobility?

# Security architecture

Security refers to the state of being free from threats and danger. Information security is the state of being safeguarded against the unwarranted use of data, particularly electronic information, or the precautions in place to accomplish this. The growing use of the internet and mobile applications has posed a great risk to information security.

The set of ad hoc actions can be modified depending on the way information security is viewed. These actions can be modified by making use of adaptive solutions, applying behavior that suits business requirements and coordinated approach to principles.

This may result in the enhancement of strategic programs and reduced budgets. Therefore, there will be an increase in businesses that implement compliance with regulations using an inclusive program.

The advantages of information security architecture may be familiar with security professionals but creating and restructuring information security architecture is a challenging activity. Information security field has sophisticated dynamics, but it needs a significant investment of human labor to create a systematic architecture.

To make sure that such a commitment can be maintained for an extended period, clearly written down rules for security experts have to be followed strictly. Industries' models and reference standards are being modified every day, but the creation of universal business-wide information security remains unpredictable. Because of these modifications, it is recommended for businesses to come up with and maintain their Information Security Architectures, by employing the use of suitable industry articles and models.

Almost 40 percent of large businesses have invested heavily in information security benefits. However, most of these investments are concerned with technology. The growth is estimated to grow to 60 percent in the following years, and the designs will be more strategic and not just centered on technology.

The following are the merits of information security architecture:

- Businesses always get a shared vision for information security across their departments from Information Security Architecture. Information security is implemented differently based on business the departments which have certain motivations and objectives.

- Executives usually take information security as part of their legal and strategic management duties. Business managers are exected by Information Security Architecture to be responsible for the integrity of their applications and data.

- Information Technology companies are required to provide security services to companies while employees are required to demonstrate good corporate citizenship. A shared vision in companies is vital, given the impact, reach, and scale of information security in all sectors of business.

- Businesses may be helped by the Information Security Architecture to align their activities, strategies, and initiatives to accomplish the common vision. This is important in

155

discouraging dormant activities in the business, promoting consistency, and increasing re-use of business resources. Consequently, there will be improved progress and speed towards the accomplishment of the shared vision.

- Information Security Architecture enhances understandable and common language for communication by coming up with simple definitions of information security. Many security terms which have been used for many years are usually commonly used outside the information security field. Besides, as the field of information security continues to change, new terminologies will come into existence.

Teamwork and cooperation are necessary to ensure that information security is useful in most businesses. Therefore, it is essential for all branches of the company to possess a shared and similar comprehension of the terms used in information security architecture.

Moreover, information security architecture helps business managers to be familiar with the nature of the language that businesses employ in communicating externally; that is, the words used by suppliers and some vendors to communicate.

Languages and definitions used in information security architecture can be challenging to understand because of the information security market. Consequently, information security architecture always gives a set of terms that can assist you to comprehend these terms.

Businesses that have applied information security architecture successfully have enjoyed many benefits. They have access to a platform that can assist them to comprehend the standard management tools, processes, and principles that are vital in implementing secure networks that are compatible with the business objectives and requirements. By doing this, businesses can select and have a perfect balance between consistency and flexibility.

Information security architecture assists business stakeholders in understanding information about regulatory compliance, risk management, and security. Majority of the regulators accept that addressing network security issues is an endless and continuous activity. The most natural and easy way to deal with such problems is to record all the activities and find out the reasons why they were recorded.

# Chapter 10: Minimum os command and example in Windows, Linux an Macos

The security of your network should not be taken for granted but should be of paramount importance to you. It is imperative that you put preventive measures in place to forestall both external and internal attacks on your network. Consider these security measures:

## Update your patches

Cybercriminals are reputable for exploiting vulnerability in software applications, operating systems, browser plug-ins, and web browsers. Thus, to prevent cybercriminals from exploiting the vulnerability, ensure that you use the latest software applications. If your software applications have automatic updating feature, enable this. You should also take an inventory of your hardware as well. Pay attention to the hardware and other devices connected to the network. Are they the latest versions with the right protection? Can they withstand attacks or will they cave in under pressure and thus serve as the loophole that will be exploited?

The updated versions of these applications and hardware are designed to rectify some of the loopholes in outdated versions that can be exploited by cyber attackers. This includes fixing bugs and other potential weaknesses in the applications. Malicious programs such as worms, Trojans, viruses, and other harmful malware are created regularly. As they are created, they are equally designed to adapt to existing security ensures and exploit any weaknesses and loopholes in system software. Thus, any existing security system implemented in your network may be effective against current malware programs. Thus, you are guaranteed by using applications that can withstand potential hackings.

## Configure your exception handling processes

There may be some error messages when your network is in operation. How you handle the errors may also have a bearing on the security of your network. A practical tip is to configure your network's exception handling processes to ensure that whatever error message that is generated is returned to the external or internal system. It may also involve preventing users from including sensitive information that attackers may find useful.

## Conduct assurance processes

Your security measure should include conducting assurance processes. To do this, you must regularly conduct penetration tests of your network's architecture as well as perform simulated cyber-attacks on the network with a view to ensure that your network can withstand attacks.

## Use strong passwords

Passwords are integral parts of a network. A couple of network components and software are usually password-protected for obvious reasons. However, passwording a component or software doesn't guarantee protection against hacking if you don't do it right. Passwording your network or its components goes beyond using random words. There are some useful tips that will help you create a very formidable and strong password for your network. Here are some tips:

- **It should be long:** This is one of the areas where a lot of people expose themselves to attacks. Out of their desire to make their passwords easy to remember, they use very short, easy-to-remember passwords. Therein lies the problem. If your password is very short and can easily be remembered, chances are that they are pretty easy to crack as well. According to cybersecurity experts, the difficulty of cracking passwords is directly proportional to the length and complexity of the password. For instance, consider these two passwords:

Password A: mynetwork

Password B: @Mypassword&2018

It is very obvious that hackers will be delighted to have to deal with Password A due to its short length and other factors noted below.

- **It should contain alphanumeric characters:** Well, this is a valuable tip that shouldn't be ignored. A strong password is not made of alphabets alone but a mixture of both alphabets and numbers, hence, alphanumeric. When you compare Password A and Password B, it is pretty obvious that the former is made up of alphabets only while the latter is a combination of alphabets and some numbers. The inclusion of the numbers increases the strength of the password and forms a more difficult to hack password.

- **Include special characters:** I'm of the opinion that you understand what a special character is. These are characters like @, $, &, !, and ^ to present a few. To increase your password strength, you should include some of these special characters in your password. They also contribute to the strength of the password, a deterrent to potential hackers. In the case study above, Password A doesn't include a single special character. That makes the user of such password a sitting duck, vulnerable to attacks. It will only take hackers a couple of minutes to circumvent the password and gain unauthorized access to the network. In sharp contrast, Password B contains some special characters such as @ and &. This makes the password stronger than its counterpart. In a nutshell, Password B ticks all the boxes – is longer, contains special characters, and is alphanumeric — and is a stronger password than Password A.

- **Change your password regularly:** According to the SANS Institute, passwords should be changed regularly. The institute recommends changing your password at least every 3 months to make it difficult for people to monitor your password.

- **Don't reuse passwords:** Reusing passwords is the greatest undoing of many people that have fallen victim of hacking. The danger lies in getting access to one of your passwords and the hacker will take over the entire network within a short time. The institute also suggests that you shouldn't reuse your last 15 passwords.

- **Don't share your password(s) indiscriminately:** If you have the habit of sharing your password(s) to every Tom, Dick, and Harry, that may turn out to be your undoing. You obviously have no idea of who will use the password for malicious intent, thereby harming both you and your network. Thus, unless it is absolutely necessary, you shouldn't share your password(s) with anyone. If you have to do it, ensure you are sharing with people with a track record of integrity, not someone with a huge question mark over his or her integrity.

- **Set up guest network access:** If you must allow visitors and friends access to your network, it is a course of wisdom to create a guest network access for them. That allows you to give them a different password from the administrator's password at your disposal.

This prevents users with malicious intent from gaining unauthorized administrator's access.

- **Consider using password manager:** A password manager can serve as a reliable storage place for your password, especially if you are using a password that is so difficult and strong that you can't easily remember it. Rather than store passwords on one of the connected devices where they can easily be stolen, a password manager is safe and easy to use.

If you want a convenient way of remembering your network password, the password manager is the right tool. You only need to remember the password to the manager. Once you unlock your account, all the previously saved passwords on the account become accessible, and you won't have to always keep a long list of passwords in unsafe places. Password managers come in three different types: online password manager services, password manager software, and password manager apps for Android and iPhone users.

Some free Android password managers are Secrets for Android and KeePassDroid. If you are an iPhone user, you have Passible, Dashlane, 1Password, and LastPass to choose from. Each of these password managers has its pros and cons that should be given much consideration before settling for it. Thus, you should do your due diligence when shopping for a password manager so you can get the password manager that meets your personal needs. A visit to the official websites of these managers will give you the information you need.

When creating passwords for your network and its components, always keep these tips in mind. This will assist you to create formidable passwords that will boost the security of your network. Sometimes, creating a password can be very challenging. You may have to struggle with the challenge of how to combine these tips to create the perfect passwords for your network without relying on random passwords. Just as there are tips that are valuable in creating strong passwords, there are also some tips that remove the stress of creating a password and makes the process pretty easy. Let's consider a few of these tips:

- Don't turn to the dictionary for your choice of word. As a rule of thumb, don't use any dictionary word. Potential hackers are literate too that use sophisticated tools that can easily pick any dictionary word used as a password.

- Avoid foreign words and proper nouns as well. You can do better than rely on these words and nouns. Remember, they have the right tools for their jobs and can easily detect these words.

- Avoid using numbers that can easily be guessed if a hacker takes a look at your email. Numbers that are derived from your date of birth, street numbers, phone numbers, social security number, and other personal information shouldn't be a part of your password. You put yourself at a great risk if you include these numbers. A peep into your email content may give you away.

- You should also avoid using anything that is remotely or closely related to your nickname, name, pets, and family members.

168

If you use words from the list above and the hackers have access to them, reaching you won't pose a challenge.

- What about choosing a phrase you can identify with? Using phrases that have meaning for you can be of help too. Make a list of these phrases and take the first word of the phrases to come up with something unique that can't be easily guessed.

When you implement these tips, you will come up with a unique password. Then, add some special characters and numbers to the newly-coined word, and you have a unique, strong, and difficult to crack a password.

## Secure your VPN

You can secure your VPN by paying attention to identity authentication and data encryption. If you keep your network connection open, you are giving hackers a vulnerability they can easily exploit to take over your network. What is more, the vulnerability of data increases as it travels over the Internet. Thus, it is important that you review the appropriate documentation for your VPN software and server to ensure that you are not using anything but the strongest protocol for authentication and encryption. Another brilliant idea is to separate your VPN network from the other parts of the network with a firewall. Thus, an attack on your network won't have any impact on your VPN.

You should also consider these tips:

- Create some user-access policies and enforce them.

- Make sure that people connected to the network can handle the security of their wireless networks without issues. Malicious software programs that have infected their devices may also infect the network if not properly handled.

- You should always check the firewalls and other security measures you put in place regularly to ensure that they are up-to-date and still effective.

If it is a company network, the following security measures will be valuable to the company:

- Compile a list of authorized software and don't allow your employees to downloading applications that are not on the list. With the assistance of software inventory applications, you can get the list.

- If the company has written security policies, update them regularly. For instance, spell out the personal devices that are allowed to have access to the network. Don't forget to state specifically how long a device should be stolen or lost before it is reported.

- You should also run vulnerability scanning tools once a week.

- Don't forget to monitor your network traffic. This will allow you to notice possible threats and unusual activity patterns that can be prevented with the right approach.

## Implement Access Control

It is important to know that not every Tom, Dick, and Harry should have unrestricted access to your network. The goal is to ensure that you have control of those who have access to the network. This is very important if you wish to keep potential attackers out of your network. If you can't recognize each device and user, your chances of being attacked will increase. With this knowledge, it becomes easier for you to enforce any security policies you have put in place.

## Data loss prevention

This is absolutely important if you are running a company or an organization. You should put a measure in place that will drastically prevent data loss. A practical solution is to prevent your staff from sending sensitive information that may be used against you by hackers outside the network. You can take the preventive measure a bit further by installing DLP (Data Loss Prevention) technologies. Thus, rest assured that the security of your data is guaranteed and that will also prevent data loss through any of the channels listed above.

The importance of this technology to the security of your network cannot be overemphasized. Sensitive data and information can end up in the wrong hands through instant messaging, email, file transfers, website forms, and other channels. With DLP strategies, you have an effective solution that can monitor the flow of information with a view to detect and block an unauthorized flow of information from the network.

DLP technologies work on a set of rules that allow them to search through electronic communications in search of sensitive information or to detect any abnormal data transfers in the network. Some of the valuable pieces of information that can be prevented from leaving the network include financial data, intellectual property, customer details, and other pieces of information that may be either intentionally or accidentally leaked. There are different DLP technologies for a variety of uses too. These are:

- **DLP for data in use:** This DLP class is effective for securing in use. This is data that an endpoint or an application is actively processing. The safeguards used here involve controlling users' access to some resources as well as authenticating users.

- **DLP for data in motion:** Sometimes, confidential data may be in transit across a network and may need to be protected in transit. This technology is needed to ensure that the data is not routed to an insecure storage area or outside the organization. One of the most effective technologies used to achieve this is encryption. Email security also plays a huge part here.

- **DLP for data at rest:** You equally need to protect a data at rest just as you deem it fit to pay attention to other data. This DLP technology is designed for protecting data residing in different storage mediums such as a cloud. DLP can effectively control access and track such data.

## Use antimalware and antivirus software

Malware is a shortened form of malicious software. This includes worms, viruses, ransomware, and the likes.

Sometimes, a network may be infected by malware without visible impact due to the ability of malware to lie dormant for a couple of days or weeks before attacking the network. In the dormant state, it plans how to attack your network and will eventually carry out its plans if it is not swiftly identified and removed.

With the best antimalware programs, you can scan your network for malware upon entry, and it prevents the entry of any malware spotted during the scan. In addition, the program will continuously scan your network for potential dangers, anomalies, and whatever can compromise the security of the network.

## Wireless security

It is a known fact that wireless networks don't boast of the same security that wired networks can boast of. If you don't put some stringent security measures in place, using a wireless network will expose you to hacking. To prevent the security weakness of your wireless network to be exploited, it is important that you fortify your network security with products that are specifically designed for protecting wireless networks.

An effective wireless security solution will guarantee:

- Rogue detection that will effectively prevent any attempt to breach the security of your network by opening unsecured holes in it

- Continuous analysis of your wireless spectrum's quality

- Scanning for mitigation and threat detection

These attributes give you the confidence that your network and other devices connected to it are well protected.

## Network Segmentation

Network segmentation is a software-defined security technology for classifying network traffic into different categories. This makes it easier for you to enforce security policies on those using the network. This classification is based on the endpoint entity and not the mere IP addresses only. The access can be assigned based on location, role, and other factors so that the right users receive the right access level while suspicious devices are prevented from gaining access to the network, making it easy to remediate the problem.

## Intrusion Prevention System

Using an Intrusion Prevention System (IPS) is a good way to give your network top-notch security. The system is designed to scan network traffic with the objective of blocking attacks. One of the best of these prevention systems is the Cisco Next-Generation system. It correlates global threat intelligence and uses the knowledge to block all malicious activities on a network in addition to tracking how suspect malware and files move across the network in order to prevent the spread of outbreaks and thus prevent reinfection as well.

## Email security

Email gateways are the most popular tool for a security breach. For years, attackers have mastered the act of using social engineering tactics and personal information for building sophisticated and effective phishing campaigns for deceiving recipients and eventually hacking their networks. You have tons of email security applications at your disposal. These applications can block incoming attacks and prevent them from wreaking havoc on your network. They are also effective for controlling outbound messages, another preventive measure against the loss of confidential and sensitive data.

## Web Security

The significance of a web security solution to your network security cannot be ignored. The right solution will control how your staff use the web, block potential threats, and generally deny them access to malicious websites. Whether you have your web gateway in the cloud or on site, the web security solution will also protect it.

## Application Security

It is imperative that you protect whatever software you run on your network. Regardless of whether the software is purchased from a third party or developed by your IT staff, ensure that they are well protected as a preventive measure against being made vulnerable to attacks by the software. For instance, it is not strange to detect vulnerabilities or holes in software programs, and hackers won't hesitate to exploit that loophole. Thus, application security includes the software, hardware, and other processes you deployed to block potential holes that can be used against your network.

## Behavioral Analytics

I once mentioned the importance of monitoring your network for signs of anomalies or irrational behavior on the network. However, this won't be possible if you have no idea what constitutes irrational behavior or what it looks like. You don't have to stress yourself thinking about how to go about it or identify abnormal behaviors. You have some effective tools, such as behavioral analytics tools, at your disposal. These tools will automatically scan your network for irregular activities that deviate from the norm. Then, your security team can take over by identifying the threat and quickly addressing it.

## Consider physical network security

This basic security measure is most at times overlooked. This technique involves keeping your network hardware well protected from physical intrusion or theft. You should know that corporations don't joke with this security measure because it is quite effective regardless of how simple it is. They spend huge sums of money to create well-guarded facilities where they lock their network switches, network servers, and other important network components.

Well, if you have your network at home or other small places, building a separate compartment for locking them up may be out of the equation. However, you can still implement this security measure. Keep your broadband routers in well-guarded and safe private locations in your home. Those places should be kept secret from guests and nosy neighbors. If you are concerned about physical theft, an effective solution is not storing your data locally. You can use online backup services for keeping sensitive files stored in safe locations that ensure the security of your data if your local hardware is compromised or stolen.

As a part of the physical network security measure, pay attention to how you use your mobile devices, especially if they are connected to a network; it is very easy to leave small gadgets behind when using them in public places or have them fall out of your pockets ignorantly. There are stories abound of people who have their smartphone and other mobile devices stolen in public. In some cases, these devices were stolen while being used. Thus, it is important that you are alert to your environment when using mobile devices.

Finally, monitor your phone whenever you loan it to someone. This precautionary measure is important because a malicious person can install monitoring software on the phone, steal your personal data, or conduct some other harmful activities that may compromise the integrity of your network if you leave him unattended for a couple of minutes. The combination of two or more of these security techniques will increase the security of your network and thus prevent the network from sudden and destructive attacks. This will ensure the continuous use of the network without the fear of losing valuable and sensitive information or data to unauthorized personnel.

# Wireless Network Security

A decade ago, computers were considered as a luxury and not a necessity. It was the exclusive property of the wealthy and lucky and a network was exclusively reserved for large organizations and corporations. However, things have changed. Nearly everyone now has access to a computer or some other Internet-enabled devices. Wireless networking technology has really made a network available for all and sundry. However, this comes at a price: insecurity. Your network can be remotely hacked while your confidential information may be stolen for a ransom (ransomware) or for some other purposes. However, with some security measures, you can fortify your wireless network's security issues and prevent hackers from exploiting you. Consider these tips:

- **Disable identifier broadcasting:** Of course, you increase your chances of getting hacked if you announce to the world that you have a wireless connection. Trust hackers to pay you an unscheduled visit. Therefore, it is an invitation to disaster if you keep your identifier broadcasting enabled. Increase your network security by disabling this feature. Check your hardware's manual to enable you to disable this feature and secure your network.

- **Restrict unnecessary traffic:** Many wireless and wired routers are equipped with built-in firewalls designed to provide a line of defense for your network. In order to understand how to take advantage of this simple security measure, read your hardware's manual and learn the best way to configure your router to give access to approved outgoing and incoming traffic only.

Combine these security measures with the ones discussed previously, and you have a solid and formidable network that can't easily be hacked.

# Chapter 11: Troubleshooting

Network Management Protocol (NMP) refers to a "suite of network protocols that define the processes, procedures and policies for managing, monitoring and maintaining a computer network." This protocol is responsible for conveying and managing the communications and operations done on a computer. It addresses a wide range of tasks designed to ensure that a network performs up to its maximum potentials. The protocol is used by a network manager for evaluating and troubleshooting the network connection between a client device and host. When the protocol is executed, the protocol will provide some important information such as the status and availability of the host. It also handles packet/data loss, network latency, errors, and other information.

The policies and procedures defined within the protocol can also be applied to network-enabled computing devices. Some computing devices that can benefit from this protocol are routers, switches, servers, and computers. Some common network management protocols are:

- **Simple Network Management Protocol (SNMP):** SNMP is currently the standard network for network management. It is a simple protocol that defines information exchange between management agents and network management applications. This is a set of protocols designed for managing and monitoring management. The protocols are supported by hubs, routers, switches, modem racks, bridges, printers, servers, and some other network devices and components.

The devices supported by the network are all items connected to the network, and it is imperative that they are monitored in order to be abreast of their conditions for appropriate, proper, and continuous network administration. The SNMP protocol makes up the application layer of another protocol, the TCP/IP, in conformity with the rules set down by the Internet Engineering Task Force. A network managed by this protocol must have these three key components: software agents, managed devices (servers, routers, switches), and a network management system.

• **Internet Control Message Protocol (ICMP):** This protocol is a TCP/IP protocol responsible for providing control and error messages and troubleshooting services. The protocol is mostly used for network computers in operating systems. The protocol allows both the hosts and gateways to report problems to the machine. The functions of the Internet Control Message Protocol are:

- Test whether a specific destination is not dead and is reachable

- Report parameter problems with a datagram header

- Obtain subnet masks and Internet addresses

- Transits time estimations in addition to performing clock synchronization

When there is a problem in the communication environment, ICMP is saddled with the responsibility of sending feedback about the problems. Some situations that may require that ICMP messages are sent include:

- When it is impossible for a packet to reach its destination

- When a gateway host cannot forward a packet because it doesn't have sufficient buffering for such task

- When a gateway has the capacity to command a host to send traffic through a shorter route

These are the top protocols that are widely used for connecting networks:

- **Bluetooth:** A Bluetooth is a network protocol primarily used for wireless networking purposes. It is usually used in mobile phones as well as other gadgets such as laptops and headsets for the transmission of different features of the gadget.

- **IP:** The IP is viewed as Internet connections' identifiers. It is also used to establish a connection between two computers.

- **Routing:** The routing protocol is widely used for computers and other devices that can be found in a router. Routing is commonly used for Internet connections.

- **HTTP:** Hypertext Transfer Protocol has a different application entirely. It works with your IP address and the Internet to connect you to a website. Without the HTTP, Internet connection is impossible.

# Site Planning and Project Management

## Project planning and requirements

After defining the project and appointing the project team, the next phase is the detailed project planning. Project planning is normally done by following the project management life cycle. It informs every person involved in the project what you intend to accomplish and how you will achieve your goals. The project plan is documented, project requirements and deliverables are defined, and the project schedule is made. It entails coming up with a set of plans to guide your team via the closure and implementation phases of the project. The plans developed during this phase will be of great help in managing quality, risk, modifications, cost, and time. They may also help you supervise staff and control suppliers to see to it that you finish the project before the deadline.

The aim of the project planning phase is:

- Coming up with the business needs
- Establishing resource plans

- Obtaining management approval before proceeding to the next phase

The fundamental processes of project planning are:

- Procurement planning

Subcontracting by concentrating on vendors external to your business

- Budget planning

You specify the budget cost to be spent on the whole project.

- Risk management

You will be tasked with planning for possible risks by taking into account mitigation strategies and contingency plans.

- Communication planning

Make use of all project stakeholders and use them to come up with the best communication strategy.

- Resource planning

You can do this by indicating who will do a certain task and the specific time for the work to be done. Also, you can indicate whether there is a need for any special skills to do the task.

- Scope planning

You should specify the in-scope needs for the project to make it easier for the work to break down the structure to be created.

- Quality planning

**It entails assessing the criteria of the quality to be used in the project.**

Network requirements

For a network to operate efficiently, three fundamentals requirements must be present: the network must provide services, connections, and communication.

- Connections-they includes the software and the hardware or physical components. The physical components connect the computer to the network. The network medium and the network interface are the two important terms of network connections. The networking hardware that connects one computer device to another is called the **network medium**.

The physical component that connects the computer to the network medium and functions as an interpreter between the network and the equipment is called the **network interface card (NIC).**

- Communication- it establishes the regulations about how computer devices exchange information and understand one another. Computers must speak a common language to communicate effectively because they run different software. In the absence of shared communication, computers cannot exchange information successfully.
- Services- they are the utilities or things that a computer shares with the network. For instance, a computer may share specific files or a printer. Unless computers connected on a network can share resources such as files and printers, they will remain isolated although they will be connected physically.

## Planning access point-placement

Accurate placement of access points is necessary to unleash the full potential and performance of wireless connections. In many enterprises, access points for local area networks primarily distributed in interior compartments. These access points were traditionally preferred and selected based on WLAN bandwidth, aesthetics, the feasibility of deployment, coverage, and channel re-use. In some instances, client preferences and deployment restrictions determine the access point placement location. For example, the placement of access points on floor perimeters may be illegal.

Note that it is not necessary to place access points precisely on the perimeter. Access points can be placed inside an apartment to offer better coverage of RF in addition to minimizing wastage of RF outside the apartment.

## Using antennae to tailor coverage

It is necessary to offer coverage for a unique region that does not follow the rules and conventions you expect it to follow. Majority of the access points use omnidirectional antennas that radiate in all directions equally. Modifying the radio coverage pattern for certain applications may be vital. This work is usually done by adjusting overage from an access point to match with a specific region or by boosting a signal to fill a hole. With the reducing cost of access points, customized tailoring coverage of antennas is not crucial as it was in the past.

Types of Antennas

All wireless NIC cards have antennas built-in internally, but they cannot be used if you plan to cover an office or any vast region such as a college or a campus. External antennas are used as access points if you plan to cover a wide area. You should pay attention to the following features when considering specialized antennas:

- Gain
- Antenna type
- Half-power beam width

194

- Vertical antennas

## 802.11 Network Analysis

Sometimes, wireless connections break. Wireless local area connection enhance productivity, but they pose a great danger of total outage because the bandwidth is often overloaded. After creating a wireless local area connection, network managers should investigate any possible problems that may be experienced by the user.

As with many types of networks, a trusty network analyzer should be used by the network engineer to identify any possibilities of the network outage. Network analyzers exist for wired networks and can still be used to troubleshoot wireless connections. For success in analyzing the wireless connections, you require to view the airwaves and also try to use a network analyzer tool that is designed specifically for the same reason.

## 802.11 Tuning of Performance

Initially, wireless network managers somehow enjoyed a free ride. Wireless is cool and new, and most clients don't know what kind of service they should wait for. Moreover, most wireless connections are dependent logically to existing wired networks. 802.11 standards were designed to add functionality to existing local area connections but not to substitute them. When the wired local area connection is the main network, clients can get the work done without the wireless network, and it is viewed as less important. Most likely, your major problems are placing your access points so you can have network coverage everywhere you desire, keeping your security configuration updated, and installing required drivers.

Even though wireless connections have a specific way of growing, and customers have a way of demanding for better services as time goes by. The performance of your network "out of the box" is always fairly poor, even if no one but you realizes. Changing the external environment (by doing experiments with external antennas and placement of access points, et cetera.) may do away with some problems, but others may be addressed better by making use of administrative factors. This section discusses in detail some of the organizational factors.

The Architecture of a Logical Wireless Network

Managing a wireless local area connection installation is an essential activity that cuts across numerous distinct professions. This section starts the discussion of wireless local area connections installation and deployment by considering the architecture of the network. Designing of a network is concerned about a balance or trade-offs among certain factors, such as performance, availability, manageability, and cost. Wireless connections are also concerned about the mobility of the network.

Such networks regularly support an existing wired connection. The wired connection may be sophisticated to start with, mainly if it covers many residences in a school setting. Wireless connections solely depend on the availability of a stable, fantastic, solid wired connection in place. If the current network in use is unstable, the probability is high that the wireless extension will fail because it may also be unstable.

This section discusses four methods for creating a wireless local area connection. All are considered based on the nature of the technical characteristics of the wireless local area connection that determines how you come up with a wireless network. In what ways do the characteristics of wireless local area connections affect the topology of the network? In addition to the 802.11 standards, what other factors and hardware are required to install a network successfully? How can the logical wireless network be built to ensure there is maximum mobility?

# Conclusion

Our lives have been changed by mobile and wireless devices in recent years and this trend will obviously continue in the future. The invention of smart homes, driverless cars, optical communication, and other technological advancements gives the assurance that the future of wireless and mobile devices is very bright. Here are some things the wireless technology industry will provide in the nearest future:

- **Free battery power:** Today, many phone users run tons of apps on a daily basis, and this can have a huge impact on the phone's battery. This is obviously the reason why you carry battery packs around to recharge your phone when you're not at home. At the moment, you can power your cell phones with solar batteries, but that's the tip of the iceberg. The future promises to be fun because you may have the option of recharging your phone with the excess heat generated by your body. MIT is taking advantage of the "energy-harvesting systems" to produce the technology that allows you to

- **Increased communication speeds:** These days, you have different information sharing techniques. The options at your disposal include fiber-optic cabling, satellite networks, full duplex communication, and free-space optics. Despite the avalanche of options to choose from, there is room for improvement. In the wireless technology industry, the new 5G Wi-Fi and the potential for an awesome transmission speed of about 1 GB/second assures users of the opportunity to receive or send information faster than the current technology transmission speed can offer.